ACCESS YOUR ONLINE RESOURCES

DON'T MISS OUT ON THE ONLINE RESOURCES INCLUDED WITH YOUR PURCHASE!

Your purchase of this product unlocks access to our Online Resources page. Elevate your study experience with our **interactive practice test interface**, along with all of the additional resources that we couldn't include in this book.

Flip to the Online Resources section at the end of this book to find the link and a QR code to get started!

TOEFL iBT®

Preparation Book 2025-2026

2 Full-Length Practice Tests

TOEFL® Secrets Study Guide with Step-by-Step Video Tutorials

Includes Audio Links for the Listening Section

Written and edited by Matthew Bowling

Printed in the United States of America

This paper meets the requirements of ANSI/NISO Z39.48-1992 (Permanence of Paper).

Mometrix offers volume discount pricing to institutions. For more information or a price quote, please contact our sales department at sales@mometrix.com or 888-248-1219.

ISBN 13: 978-1-5167-2824-4
ISBN 1-5167-2824-6

Dear Future Exam Success Story

First of all, **THANK YOU** for purchasing Mometrix study materials!

Second, congratulations! You are one of the few determined test-takers who are committed to doing whatever it takes to excel on your exam. **You have come to the right place.** We developed these study materials with one goal in mind: to deliver you the information you need in a format that's concise and easy to use.

In addition to optimizing your guide for the content of the test, we've outlined our recommended steps for breaking down the preparation process into small, attainable goals so you can make sure you stay on track.

We've also analyzed the entire test-taking process, identifying the most common pitfalls and showing how you can overcome them and be ready for any curveball the test throws you.

Standardized testing is one of the biggest obstacles on your road to success, which only increases the importance of doing well in the high-pressure, high-stakes environment of test day. Your results on this test could have a significant impact on your future, and this guide provides the information and practical advice to help you achieve your full potential on test day.

Your success is our success

We would love to hear from you! If you would like to share the story of your exam success or if you have any questions or comments in regard to our products, please contact us at **800-673-8175** or **support@mometrix.com**.

Thanks again for your business and we wish you continued success!

Sincerely,
The Mometrix Test Preparation Team

Table of Contents

Introduction

Thank you for purchasing this resource! You have made the choice to prepare yourself for a test that could have a huge impact on your future, and this guide is designed to help you be fully ready for test day. Obviously, it's important to have a solid understanding of the test material, but you also need to be prepared for the unique environment and stressors of the test, so that you can perform to the best of your abilities.

For this purpose, the first section that appears in this guide is the **Secret Keys**. We've devoted countless hours to meticulously researching what works and what doesn't, and we've boiled down our findings to the five most impactful steps you can take to improve your performance on the test. We start at the beginning with study planning and move through the preparation process, all the way to the testing strategies that will help you get the most out of what you know when you're finally sitting in front of the test.

We recommend that you start preparing for your test as far in advance as possible. However, if you've bought this guide as a last-minute study resource and only have a few days before your test, we recommend that you skip over the first two Secret Keys since they address a long-term study plan.

If you struggle with **test anxiety**, we strongly encourage you to check out our recommendations for how you can overcome it. Test anxiety is a formidable foe, but it can be beaten, and we want to make sure you have the tools you need to defeat it.

Secret Key #1 – Plan Big, Study Small

There's a lot riding on your performance. If you want to ace this test, you're going to need to keep your skills sharp and the material fresh in your mind. You need a plan that lets you review everything you need to know while still fitting in your schedule. We'll break this strategy down into three categories.

Information Organization

Start with the information you already have: the official test outline. From this, you can make a complete list of all the concepts you need to cover before the test. Organize these concepts into groups that can be studied together, and create a list of any related vocabulary you need to learn so you can brush up on any difficult terms. You'll want to keep this vocabulary list handy once you actually start studying since you may need to add to it along the way.

Time Management

Once you have your set of study concepts, decide how to spread them out over the time you have left before the test. Break your study plan into small, clear goals so you have a manageable task for each day and know exactly what you're doing. Then just focus on one small step at a time. When you manage your time this way, you don't need to spend hours at a time studying. Studying a small block of content for a short period each day helps you retain information better and avoid stressing over how much you have left to do. You can relax knowing that you have a plan to cover everything in time. In order for this strategy to be effective though, you have to start studying early and stick to your schedule. Avoid the exhaustion and futility that comes from last-minute cramming!

Study Environment

The environment you study in has a big impact on your learning. Studying in a coffee shop, while probably more enjoyable, is not likely to be as fruitful as studying in a quiet room. It's important to keep distractions to a minimum. You're only planning to study for a short block of time, so make the most of it. Don't pause to check your phone or get up to find a snack. It's also important to **avoid multitasking**. Research has consistently shown that multitasking will make your studying dramatically less effective. Your study area should also be comfortable and well-lit so you don't have the distraction of straining your eyes or sitting on an uncomfortable chair.

The time of day you study is also important. You want to be rested and alert. Don't wait until just before bedtime. Study when you'll be most likely to comprehend and remember. Even better, if you know what time of day your test will be, set that time aside for study. That way your brain will be used to working on that subject at that specific time and you'll have a better chance of recalling information.

Finally, it can be helpful to team up with others who are studying for the same test. Your actual studying should be done in as isolated an environment as possible, but the work of organizing the information and setting up the study plan can be divided up. In between study sessions, you can discuss with your teammates the concepts that you're all studying and quiz each other on the details. Just be sure that your teammates are as serious about the test as you are. If you find that your study time is being replaced with social time, you might need to find a new team.

Secret Key #2 – Make Your Studying Count

You're devoting a lot of time and effort to preparing for this test, so you want to be absolutely certain it will pay off. This means doing more than just reading the content and hoping you can remember it on test day. It's important to make every minute of study count. There are two main areas you can focus on to make your studying count.

Retention

It doesn't matter how much time you study if you can't remember the material. You need to make sure you are retaining the concepts. To check your retention of the information you're learning, try recalling it at later times with minimal prompting. Try carrying around flashcards and glance at one or two from time to time or ask a friend who's also studying for the test to quiz you.

To enhance your retention, look for ways to put the information into practice so that you can apply it rather than simply recalling it. If you're using the information in practical ways, it will be much easier to remember. Similarly, it helps to solidify a concept in your mind if you're not only reading it to yourself but also explaining it to someone else. Ask a friend to let you teach them about a concept you're a little shaky on (or speak aloud to an imaginary audience if necessary). As you try to summarize, define, give examples, and answer your friend's questions, you'll understand the concepts better and they will stay with you longer. Finally, step back for a big picture view and ask yourself how each piece of information fits with the whole subject. When you link the different concepts together and see them working together as a whole, it's easier to remember the individual components.

Finally, practice showing your work on any multi-step problems, even if you're just studying. Writing out each step you take to solve a problem will help solidify the process in your mind, and you'll be more likely to remember it during the test.

Modality

Modality simply refers to the means or method by which you study. Choosing a study modality that fits your own individual learning style is crucial. No two people learn best in exactly the same way, so it's important to know your strengths and use them to your advantage.

For example, if you learn best by visualization, focus on visualizing a concept in your mind and draw an image or a diagram. Try color-coding your notes, illustrating them, or creating symbols that will trigger your mind to recall a learned concept. If you learn best by hearing or discussing information, find a study partner who learns the same way or read aloud to yourself. Think about how to put the information in your own words. Imagine that you are giving a lecture on the topic and record yourself so you can listen to it later.

For any learning style, flashcards can be helpful. Organize the information so you can take advantage of spare moments to review. Underline key words or phrases. Use different colors for different categories. Mnemonic devices (such as creating a short list in which every item starts with the same letter) can also help with retention. Find what works best for you and use it to store the information in your mind most effectively and easily.

Secret Key #3 – Practice the Right Way

Your success on test day depends not only on how many hours you put into preparing, but also on whether you prepared the right way. It's good to check along the way to see if your studying is paying off. One of the most effective ways to do this is by taking practice tests to evaluate your progress. Practice tests are useful because they show exactly where you need to improve. Every time you take a practice test, pay special attention to these three groups of questions:

- The questions you got wrong
- The questions you had to guess on, even if you guessed right
- The questions you found difficult or slow to work through

This will show you exactly what your weak areas are, and where you need to devote more study time. Ask yourself why each of these questions gave you trouble. Was it because you didn't understand the material? Was it because you didn't remember the vocabulary? Do you need more repetitions on this type of question to build speed and confidence? Dig into those questions and figure out how you can strengthen your weak areas as you go back to review the material.

Additionally, many practice tests have a section explaining the answer choices. It can be tempting to read the explanation and think that you now have a good understanding of the concept. However, an explanation likely only covers part of the question's broader context. Even if the explanation makes perfect sense, **go back and investigate** every concept related to the question until you're positive you have a thorough understanding.

As you go along, keep in mind that the practice test is just that: practice. Memorizing these questions and answers will not be very helpful on the actual test because it is unlikely to have any of the same exact questions. If you only know the right answers to the sample questions, you won't be prepared for the real thing. **Study the concepts** until you understand them fully, and then you'll be able to answer any question that shows up on the test.

It's important to wait on the practice tests until you're ready. If you take a test on your first day of study, you may be overwhelmed by the amount of material covered and how much you need to learn. Work up to it gradually.

On test day, you'll need to be prepared for answering questions, managing your time, and using the test-taking strategies you've learned. It's a lot to balance, like a mental marathon that will have a big impact on your future. Like training for a marathon, you'll need to start slowly and work your way up. When test day arrives, you'll be ready.

Start with the strategies you've read in the first two Secret Keys—plan your course and study in the way that works best for you. If you have time, consider using multiple study resources to get different approaches to the same concepts. It can be helpful to see difficult concepts from more than one angle. Then find a good source for practice tests. Many times, the test website will suggest potential study resources or provide sample tests.

Practice Test Strategy

If you're able to find at least three practice tests, we recommend this strategy:

UNTIMED AND OPEN-BOOK PRACTICE

Take the first test with no time constraints and with your notes and study guide handy. Take your time and focus on applying the strategies you've learned.

TIMED AND OPEN-BOOK PRACTICE

Take the second practice test open-book as well, but set a timer and practice pacing yourself to finish in time.

TIMED AND CLOSED-BOOK PRACTICE

Take any other practice tests as if it were test day. Set a timer and put away your study materials. Sit at a table or desk in a quiet room, imagine yourself at the testing center, and answer questions as quickly and accurately as possible.

Keep repeating timed and closed-book tests on a regular basis until you run out of practice tests or it's time for the actual test. Your mind will be ready for the schedule and stress of test day, and you'll be able to focus on recalling the material you've learned.

Secret Key #4 – Pace Yourself

Once you're fully prepared for the material on the test, your biggest challenge on test day will be managing your time. Just knowing that the clock is ticking can make you panic even if you have plenty of time left. Work on pacing yourself so you can build confidence against the time constraints of the exam. Pacing is a difficult skill to master, especially in a high-pressure environment, so **practice is vital**.

Set time expectations for your pace based on how much time is available. For example, if a section has 60 questions and the time limit is 30 minutes, you know you have to average 30 seconds or less per question in order to answer them all. Although 30 seconds is the hard limit, set 25 seconds per question as your goal, so you reserve extra time to spend on harder questions. When you budget extra time for the harder questions, you no longer have any reason to stress when those questions take longer to answer.

Don't let this time expectation distract you from working through the test at a calm, steady pace, but keep it in mind so you don't spend too much time on any one question. Recognize that taking extra time on one question you don't understand may keep you from answering two that you do understand later in the test. If your time limit for a question is up and you're still not sure of the answer, mark it and move on, and come back to it later if the time and the test format allow. If the testing format doesn't allow you to return to earlier questions, just make an educated guess; then put it out of your mind and move on.

On the easier questions, be careful not to rush. It may seem wise to hurry through them so you have more time for the challenging ones, but it's not worth missing one if you know the concept and just didn't take the time to read the question fully. Work efficiently but make sure you understand the question and have looked at all of the answer choices, since more than one may seem right at first.

Even if you're paying attention to the time, you may find yourself a little behind at some point. You should speed up to get back on track, but do so wisely. Don't panic; just take a few seconds less on each question until you're caught up. Don't guess without thinking, but do look through the answer choices and eliminate any you know are wrong. If you can get down to two choices, it is often worthwhile to guess from those. Once you've chosen an answer, move on and don't dwell on any that you skipped or had to hurry through. If a question was taking too long, chances are it was one of the harder ones, so you weren't as likely to get it right anyway.

On the other hand, if you find yourself getting ahead of schedule, it may be beneficial to slow down a little. The more quickly you work, the more likely you are to make a careless mistake that will affect your score. You've budgeted time for each question, so don't be afraid to spend that time. Practice an efficient but careful pace to get the most out of the time you have.

Secret Key #5 – Have a Plan for Guessing

When you're taking the test, you may find yourself stuck on a question. Some of the answer choices seem better than others, but you don't see the one answer choice that is obviously correct. What do you do?

The scenario described above is very common, yet most test takers have not effectively prepared for it. Developing and practicing a plan for guessing may be one of the single most effective uses of your time as you get ready for the exam.

In developing your plan for guessing, there are three questions to address:

- When should you start the guessing process?
- How should you narrow down the choices?
- Which answer should you choose?

When to Start the Guessing Process

Unless your plan for guessing is to select C every time (which, despite its merits, is not what we recommend), you need to leave yourself enough time to apply your answer elimination strategies. Since you have a limited amount of time for each question, that means that if you're going to give yourself the best shot at guessing correctly, you have to decide quickly whether or not you will guess.

Of course, the best-case scenario is that you don't have to guess at all, so first, see if you can answer the question based on your knowledge of the subject and basic reasoning skills. Focus on the key words in the question and try to jog your memory of related topics. Give yourself a chance to bring the knowledge to mind, but once you realize that you don't have (or you can't access) the knowledge you need to answer the question, it's time to start the guessing process.

It's almost always better to start the guessing process too early than too late. It only takes a few seconds to remember something and answer the question from knowledge. Carefully eliminating wrong answer choices takes longer. Plus, going through the process of eliminating answer choices can actually help jog your memory.

Summary: Start the guessing process as soon as you decide that you can't answer the question based on your knowledge.

How to Narrow Down the Choices

The next chapter in this book (**Test-Taking Strategies**) includes a wide range of strategies for how to approach questions and how to look for answer choices to eliminate. You will definitely want to read those carefully, practice them, and figure out which ones work best for you. Here though, we're going to address a mindset rather than a particular strategy.

Your odds of guessing an answer correctly depend on how many options you are choosing from.

Number of options left	5	4	3	2	1
Odds of guessing correctly	20%	25%	33%	50%	100%

You can see from this chart just how valuable it is to be able to eliminate incorrect answers and make an educated guess, but there are two things that many test takers do that cause them to miss out on the benefits of guessing:

- Accidentally eliminating the correct answer
- Selecting an answer based on an impression

We'll look at the first one here, and the second one in the next section.

To avoid accidentally eliminating the correct answer, we recommend a thought exercise called **the $5 challenge**. In this challenge, you only eliminate an answer choice from contention if you are willing to bet $5 on it being wrong. Why $5? Five dollars is a small but not insignificant amount of money. It's an amount you could afford to lose but wouldn't want to throw away. And while losing $5 once might not hurt too much, doing it twenty times will set you back $100. In the same way, each small decision you make—eliminating a choice here, guessing on a question there—won't by itself impact your score very much, but when you put them all together, they can make a big difference. By holding each answer choice elimination decision to a higher standard, you can reduce the risk of accidentally eliminating the correct answer.

The $5 challenge can also be applied in a positive sense: If you are willing to bet $5 that an answer choice *is* correct, go ahead and mark it as correct.

Summary: Only eliminate an answer choice if you are willing to bet $5 that it is wrong.

Which Answer to Choose

You're taking the test. You've run into a hard question and decided you'll have to guess. You've eliminated all the answer choices you're willing to bet $5 on. Now you have to pick an answer. Why do we even need to talk about this? Why can't you just pick whichever one you feel like when the time comes?

The answer to these questions is that if you don't come into the test with a plan, you'll rely on your impression to select an answer choice, and if you do that, you risk falling into a trap. The test writers know that everyone who takes their test will be guessing on some of the questions, so they intentionally write wrong answer choices to seem plausible. You still have to pick an answer though, and if the wrong answer choices are designed to look right, how can you ever be sure that you're not falling for their trap? The best solution we've found to this dilemma is to take the decision out of your hands entirely. Here is the process we recommend:

Once you've eliminated any choices that you are confident (willing to bet $5) are wrong, select the first remaining choice as your answer.

Whether you choose to select the first remaining choice, the second, or the last, the important thing is that you use some preselected standard. Using this approach guarantees that you will not be enticed into selecting an answer choice that looks right, because you are not basing your decision on how the answer choices look.

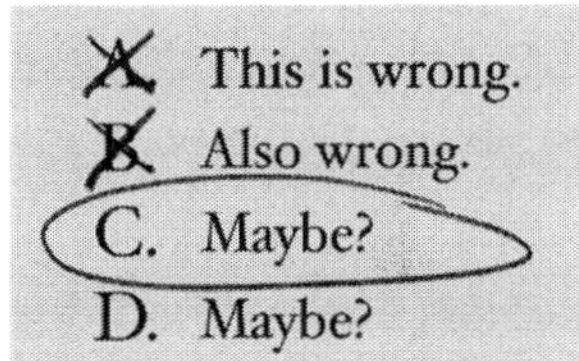

This is not meant to make you question your knowledge. Instead, it is to help you recognize the difference between your knowledge and your impressions. There's a huge difference between thinking an answer is right because of what you know, and thinking an answer is right because it looks or sounds like it should be right.

Summary: To ensure that your selection is appropriately random, make a predetermined selection from among all answer choices you have not eliminated.

Test-Taking Strategies

This section contains a list of test-taking strategies that you may find helpful as you work through the test. By taking what you know and applying logical thought, you can maximize your chances of answering any question correctly!

It is very important to realize that every question is different and every person is different: no single strategy will work on every question, and no single strategy will work for every person. That's why we've included all of them here, so you can try them out and determine which ones work best for different types of questions and which ones work best for you.

Question Strategies

☑ Read Carefully

Read the question and the answer choices carefully. Don't miss the question because you misread the terms. You have plenty of time to read each question thoroughly and make sure you understand what is being asked. Yet a happy medium must be attained, so don't waste too much time. You must read carefully and efficiently.

☑ Contextual Clues

Look for contextual clues. If the question includes a word you are not familiar with, look at the immediate context for some indication of what the word might mean. Contextual clues can often give you all the information you need to decipher the meaning of an unfamiliar word. Even if you can't determine the meaning, you may be able to narrow down the possibilities enough to make a solid guess at the answer to the question.

☑ Prefixes

If you're having trouble with a word in the question or answer choices, try dissecting it. Take advantage of every clue that the word might include. Prefixes can be a huge help. Usually, they allow you to determine a basic meaning. *Pre-* means before, *post-* means after, *pro-* is positive, *de-* is negative. From prefixes, you can get an idea of the general meaning of the word and try to put it into context.

☑ Hedge Words

Watch out for critical hedge words, such as *likely, may, can, often, almost, mostly, usually, generally, rarely*, and *sometimes*. Question writers insert these hedge phrases to cover every possibility. Often an answer choice will be wrong simply because it leaves no room for exception. Be on guard for answer choices that have definitive words such as *exactly* and *always*.

☑ Switchback Words

Stay alert for *switchbacks*. These are the words and phrases frequently used to alert you to shifts in thought. The most common switchback words are *but, although*, and *however*. Others include *nevertheless, on the other hand, even though, while, in spite of, despite*, and *regardless of*. Switchback words are important to catch because they can change the direction of the question or an answer choice.

⊘ Face Value

When in doubt, use common sense. Accept the situation in the problem at face value. Don't read too much into it. These problems will not require you to make wild assumptions. If you have to go beyond creativity and warp time or space in order to have an answer choice fit the question, then you should move on and consider the other answer choices. These are normal problems rooted in reality. The applicable relationship or explanation may not be readily apparent, but it is there for you to figure out. Use your common sense to interpret anything that isn't clear.

Answer Choice Strategies

⊘ Answer Selection

The most thorough way to pick an answer choice is to identify and eliminate wrong answers until only one is left, then confirm it is the correct answer. Sometimes an answer choice may immediately seem right, but be careful. The test writers will usually put more than one reasonable answer choice on each question, so take a second to read all of them and make sure that the other choices are not equally obvious. As long as you have time left, it is better to read every answer choice than to pick the first one that looks right without checking the others.

⊘ Answer Choice Families

An answer choice family consists of two (in rare cases, three) answer choices that are very similar in construction and cannot all be true at the same time. If you see two answer choices that are direct opposites or parallels, one of them is usually the correct answer. For instance, if one answer choice says that quantity *x* increases and another either says that quantity *x* decreases (opposite) or says that quantity *y* increases (parallel), then those answer choices would fall into the same family. An answer choice that doesn't match the construction of the answer choice family is more likely to be incorrect. Most questions will not have answer choice families, but when they do appear, you should be prepared to recognize them.

⊘ Eliminate Answers

Eliminate answer choices as soon as you realize they are wrong, but make sure you consider all possibilities. If you are eliminating answer choices and realize that the last one you are left with is also wrong, don't panic. Start over and consider each choice again. There may be something you missed the first time that you will realize on the second pass.

⊘ Avoid Fact Traps

Don't be distracted by an answer choice that is factually true but doesn't answer the question. You are looking for the choice that answers the question. Stay focused on what the question is asking for so you don't accidentally pick an answer that is true but incorrect. Always go back to the question and make sure the answer choice you've selected actually answers the question and is not merely a true statement.

⊘ Extreme Statements

In general, you should avoid answers that put forth extreme actions as standard practice or proclaim controversial ideas as established fact. An answer choice that states the "process should be used in certain situations, if..." is much more likely to be correct than one that states the "process should be discontinued completely." The first is a calm rational statement and doesn't even make a definitive, uncompromising stance, using a hedge word *if* to provide wiggle room, whereas the second choice is far more extreme.

⊘ BENCHMARK

As you read through the answer choices and you come across one that seems to answer the question well, mentally select that answer choice. This is not your final answer, but it's the one that will help you evaluate the other answer choices. The one that you selected is your benchmark or standard for judging each of the other answer choices. Every other answer choice must be compared to your benchmark. That choice is correct until proven otherwise by another answer choice beating it. If you find a better answer, then that one becomes your new benchmark. Once you've decided that no other choice answers the question as well as your benchmark, you have your final answer.

⊘ PREDICT THE ANSWER

Before you even start looking at the answer choices, it is often best to try to predict the answer. When you come up with the answer on your own, it is easier to avoid distractions and traps because you will know exactly what to look for. The right answer choice is unlikely to be word-for-word what you came up with, but it should be a close match. Even if you are confident that you have the right answer, you should still take the time to read each option before moving on.

General Strategies

⊘ TOUGH QUESTIONS

If you are stumped on a problem or it appears too hard or too difficult, don't waste time. Move on! Remember though, if you can quickly check for obviously incorrect answer choices, your chances of guessing correctly are greatly improved. Before you completely give up, at least try to knock out a couple of possible answers. Eliminate what you can and then guess at the remaining answer choices before moving on.

⊘ CHECK YOUR WORK

Since you will probably not know every term listed and the answer to every question, it is important that you get credit for the ones that you do know. Don't miss any questions through careless mistakes. If at all possible, try to take a second to look back over your answer selection and make sure you've selected the correct answer choice and haven't made a costly careless mistake (such as marking an answer choice that you didn't mean to mark). This quick double check should more than pay for itself in caught mistakes for the time it costs.

⊘ PACE YOURSELF

It's easy to be overwhelmed when you're looking at a page full of questions; your mind is confused and full of random thoughts, and the clock is ticking down faster than you would like. Calm down and maintain the pace that you have set for yourself. Especially as you get down to the last few minutes of the test, don't let the small numbers on the clock make you panic. As long as you are on track by monitoring your pace, you are guaranteed to have time for each question.

⊘ DON'T RUSH

It is very easy to make errors when you are in a hurry. Maintaining a fast pace in answering questions is pointless if it makes you miss questions that you would have gotten right otherwise. Test writers like to include distracting information and wrong answers that seem right. Taking a little extra time to avoid careless mistakes can make all the difference in your test score. Find a pace that allows you to be confident in the answers that you select.

⊘ Keep Moving

Panicking will not help you pass the test, so do your best to stay calm and keep moving. Taking deep breaths and going through the answer elimination steps you practiced can help to break through a stress barrier and keep your pace.

Final Notes

The combination of a solid foundation of content knowledge and the confidence that comes from practicing your plan for applying that knowledge is the key to maximizing your performance on test day. As your foundation of content knowledge is built up and strengthened, you'll find that the strategies included in this chapter become more and more effective in helping you quickly sift through the distractions and traps of the test to isolate the correct answer.

Now that you're preparing to move forward into the test content chapters of this book, be sure to keep your goal in mind. As you read, think about how you will be able to apply this information on the test. If you've already seen sample questions for the test and you have an idea of the question format and style, try to come up with questions of your own that you can answer based on what you're reading. This will give you valuable practice applying your knowledge in the same ways you can expect to on test day.

Good luck and good studying!

Reading

The Reading section of the TOEFL consists of a total of 20 questions which will last 35 minutes.

There are two passages, which will each be followed by ten questions each. The passages come from a variety of academic subjects at the introductory university level of difficulty.

Tips for the Reading Section

The reading section requires you to demonstrate your ability to find information, use basic comprehension, and read to learn.

Tip 1: Reading to Find Information

When reading to find specific ideas, it is important to be able to **scan** or **skim** a text for a specific phrase or context. To improve your reading speed and ability to scan a text, find passages that discuss a specific topic and practice looking for main ideas quickly without taking the time to read every word or sentence.

Tip 2: Basic Comprehension

When reading for basic comprehension of a passage, you will likely be asked to identify **themes, main ideas, and vocabulary** in context. These pieces of information are most likely to be found in the first sentence of the paragraph and in introductory or conclusion paragraphs. Spend some time reading through paragraphs and short stories looking for key information.

Tip 3: Reading to Learn

When reading to learn, one must be aware of **organization** and **presentation** of information within a passage. As you read through passages, try to identify the point of a passage, as well as whether it is speaking in an informative or persuasive manner. Keep track of important details, as some questions may require you to insert sentences that fit best in a passage. In these questions, there may be more than one answer that is technically correct, but only one that is truly the best fit.

Reading Comprehension Skills

This section is organized to introduce you to the passages that you will find on your exam. We cover the different types of passages from narrative to persuasive. Then, we move to the reason that a passage is written. As you may know, some texts are written to persuade. Other passages want to inform.

The writing devices used by writers are important to understand as you practice reading passages. The other parts of a passage we focus on are main ideas, supporting details, and themes. Then, we review making inferences and drawing conclusions. With this step-by-step guide, you will move to a higher score on your test.

Careful reading and thinking about a passage are important in every part of life. Work with this information by reading books, magazines, or newspapers. When you read carefully, you can use this information for other passages. With practice you will strengthen your skills for the future.

Types of Passages

A **narrative** passage is a story that can be fiction or nonfiction (i.e., false or true). To be a narrative, the passage must have a few things. First, the text must have a plot (i.e., an order of events). Some narratives are written in a clear order, but this is not necessary. If the narrative is good, then you will find the events interesting, regardless of the order in which they happen. Second, a narrative has characters. These characters can be people, animals, or even lifeless items. As long as they play in the plot, they are a character. Third, a narrative passage often has figurative language. This is a tool that authors use to stir the imagination of readers with comparisons or comments. For example, a metaphor is a comparison between two things without using the words *like* or *as*. *He stood like a king* is not an example of a metaphor. *The moon was a frosty snowball* is an example of a metaphor. In reality, the moon is not a snowball. Yet, the comparison gives a sense of calm to readers.

An **expository** passage aims to inform or teach readers. This type of passage is nonfiction and usually centers around an easily explained topic. Often, an expository passage has helpful organizing words: *first*, *next*, *for example*, and *therefore*. These words let readers know where they are in the passage. While expository passages don't need to have difficult vocabulary and fancy writing, they can be better with them. Yet, this can make it difficult to pay attention to an expository passage. Expository passages are not always about things that will interest you. Also, writers focus more on clearness and precision than with keeping the reader's interest. By careful reading, you will establish a good habit of focus when you read an expository passage.

Review Video: Expository Passages
Visit mometrix.com/academy and enter code: 256515

A **technical** passage is written to describe a complicated thing or action. Technical writing is common in medical and technology fields. In those fields, ideas of mathematics, science, and engineering need to be explained simply and clearly. A technical passage usually proceeds in a step-by-step order to help with understanding the passage. Technical passages often have clear headings and subheadings. These headings act like the organizing words in an expository passage: they let readers know where they are in a passage. Also, you will find that these passages divide sections by numbers or letters. Many technical passages look more like an outline than the paragraphs that you are reading right now. Depending on the audience, the amount of difficult vocabulary will change in a technical passage. Some technical passages try to stay away from language that readers will have to look up. However, some difficult vocabulary has to be used for writers to share their message.

Review Video: Technical Passages
Visit mometrix.com/academy and enter code: 478923

A **persuasive** passage is written to change the minds of readers so that they agree with the author. The purpose of the passage may be very clear or very difficult to find. A persuasive passage wants to make an acceptable argument and win the trust of the reader. In some cases, a persuasive passage will be similar to an informative passage. Both passages make an argument and offer supporting details. However, a persuasive passage is more likely to appeal to the reader's feelings and make arguments based on opinions. Persuasive passages may not describe other points of view. So, when they do show other points of view, they may show favoritism to one side.

Persuasive passages will focus on one main argument and make many minor arguments (i.e., arguments that help the main argument) along the way. If you are going to accept the main argument, then you need to accept the minor arguments. So, the main argument will only be as strong as the minor arguments. These arguments should be rooted in fact and experience, not opinions. The best persuasive passages give enough supporting detail to back up arguments without confusing readers. Remember that a fact must be open to independent verification (i.e., the fact must be something that can be backed up by someone else). Also, statistics (i.e., data or figures collected for study) are helpful only when they look at other choices. For example, a statistic on the number of bicycles sold would only be useful if it was taken over a limited time period and in a specific area. Good readers are careful with statistics because statistics can show what we want to see. Or, they can hide what we don't want to see. The writers of your test know that their passages will be met by questioning readers. So, your skill at questioning what you read will be a help in your exam.

Review Video: How to Write a Persuasive Essay
Visit mometrix.com/academy and enter code: 621428

Opinions come from how we feel and what we think. Persuasive writers often try to appeal to the emotions (i.e., use or influence someone's feelings) of readers to make their arguments. You should always ask questions about this approach. You should ask questions because an author can pull you into accepting something that you don't want to accept. Sometimes these appeals can be used fairly. For example, some subjects cannot be totally addressed without an appeal to a reader's feelings. Think about an article on drunk driving. Some examples in the article will alarm or sadden readers because of the terrible outcome.

On the other hand, appeals to feelings are unacceptable when they try to **mislead** readers. For example, a presidential candidate (i.e., someone running for president) says that he/she cares about the country. The candidate pushes you to make a connection. You care about the country as well and have positive feelings toward it. The candidate wants you to connect your positive feelings about the country with your thoughts about him or her. If you make more connections with the candidate, then you are likely to vote for him or her. Also, the person running for president hints that other candidates do not care about the country.

Another common and unacceptable appeal to feelings is the use of **loaded language**. Calling a religious person a *fanatic* or a person interested in the environment a *tree hugger* are examples of loaded language.

ORGANIZATION OF THE PASSAGE

The way a passage is organized can help readers to understand the author's purpose and conclusions. There are many ways to organize a passage, and each one has an important use.

Some nonfiction texts are organized to present a **problem** followed by a **solution**. For this type of passage, the problem is explained before the solution is given. When the problem is well known, the solution may be given in a few sentences at the beginning. Other passages may focus on the solution, and the problem will be talked about a few times. Some passages will outline many solutions to a problem. This will leave you to choose among the possible solutions. If authors have loyalty to one solution, they may not describe some of the other solutions. Be careful with the author's plan when reading a problem-solution passage. When you know the author's point of view, you can make a better judgment of the solution.

Sometimes authors will organize information clearly for you to follow and locate the information. However, this is not always the case with passages in an exam. Two common ways to order a passage are cause and effect and chronological order. When using **chronological order** (i.e., a plan that moves in order from the first step to the last), the author gives information in the order that the event happened. For example, biographies are written in chronological order. The person's birth and childhood are first. Their adult life is next. The events leading up to the person's death are last.

In **cause and effect** passages, an author shows one thing that makes something else happen. For example, if one were to go to bed very late and wake up very early, then they would be tired in the morning. The cause is a lack of sleep, with the effect of being tired the next day.

Finding the cause-and-effect relationships in a passage can be tricky. Often, these relationships come with certain words or terms. When authors use words like *because*, *since*, *in order*, and *so*, they are describing a cause and effect relationship. Think about the sentence: *He called her because he needed the homework*. This is a simple causal relationship. The cause was his need for the homework, and the effect was his phone call. Yet, not all cause and effect relationships are marked like this. Think about the sentences: *He called her. He needed the homework.* When the cause-and-effect relationship does not come with a keyword, the relationship can be known by asking why. For example, *He called her.* Why did he call her? The answer is in the next sentence: He needed the homework.

Review Video: Rhetorical Strategy of Cause-and-Effect Analysis
Visit mometrix.com/academy and enter code: 725944

When authors try to change the minds of readers, they may use cause-and-effect relationships. However, these relationships should not always be taken at face value. To read a persuasive essay well, you need to judge the cause-and-effect relationships. For example, imagine an author wrote the following: *The parking deck has not been making money because people want to ride their bikes.* The relationship is clear: the cause is that people want to ride their bikes. The effect is that the parking deck has not been making money. However, you should look at this argument again. Maybe there are other reasons that the parking deck was not a success: a bad economy, too many costs, etc.

Many passages follow the **compare-and-contrast** model. In this model, the similarities and differences between two ideas or things are reviewed. A review of the similarities between ideas is called comparison. In a perfect comparison, the author shows ideas or things in the same way. If authors want to show the similarities between football and baseball, they can list the equipment and rules for each game. Think about the similarities as they appear in the passage and take note of any differences.

Review Video: Compare and Contrast
Visit mometrix.com/academy and enter code: 798319

Careful thinking about ideas and conclusions can seem like a difficult task. You can make this task easy by understanding the basic parts of ideas and writing skills. Looking at the way that ideas link to others is a good way to begin. Sometimes authors will write about two opposing ideas. Other times, an author will support a topic, and another author will argue against the topic. The review of these rival ideas is known as **contrast**. In contrast, all ideas should be presented clearly. If the author does favor a side, you need to read carefully to find how the author shows or hides this favoritism. Also, as you read the passage, you should write out how one side views the other.

Purposes for Writing

To be a careful reader, pay attention to the author's **position** and purpose. Even passages that seem fair and equal--like textbooks--have a position or bias (i.e., the author is unfair or inaccurate with opposing ideas). Readers need to take these positions into account when considering the author's message. Authors who appeal to feelings or favor one side of an argument make their position clear. Authors' positions may be found in what they write and in what they don't write. Normally, you would want to review other passages on the same topic to understand the author's position. However, you are in the middle of an exam. So, look for language and arguments that show a position.

Review Video: Author's Position
Visit mometrix.com/academy and enter code: 827954

Sometimes, finding the **purpose** of an author is easier than finding his or her position. In most cases, the author has no interest in hiding his or her purpose. A passage for entertainment will be written to please readers. Most stories are written to entertain. However, they can inform or persuade. Informative texts are easy to recognize. The most difficult purpose of a text to determine is persuasion. In persuasion, the author wants to make the purpose hard to find. When you learn that the author wants to persuade, you should be skeptical of the argument. Persuasive passages may try to establish an entertaining tone and hope to amuse you into agreement. On the other hand, an informative tone may be used to seem fair and equal to all sides.

An author's purpose is clear often in the organization of the text (e.g., section headings in bold font point to an informative passage). However, you may not have this organization in your passages. So, if authors make their main idea clear from the beginning, then their likely purpose is to inform. If the author makes a main argument and gives minor arguments for support, then the purpose is probably to persuade. If the author tells a story, then his or her purpose is most likely to entertain. If the author wants your attention more than to persuade or inform, then his or her purpose is most likely to entertain. You must judge authors on how well they reach their purpose. In other words, think about the type of passage (e.g., technical, persuasive, etc.) that the author has written and if the author has followed the demands of the passage type.

Review Video: Understanding the Author's Intent
Visit mometrix.com/academy and enter code: 511819

The author's purpose will influence his or her writing approach and the reader's reaction. In a **persuasive essay**, the author wants to prove something to readers. There are several important marks of bad persuasive writing. Opinion given as fact is one mark. When some authors try to persuade readers, they give their opinions as if they were facts. Readers must be on guard for statements that sound like facts but cannot be tested. Another mark of persuasive writing is the appeal to feelings. An author will try to play with the feelings of readers by appealing to their ideas of what is right and wrong. When an author uses strong language to excite the reader's feelings, then the author may want to persuade. Many times, a persuasive passage will give an unfair explanation of other sides. Or, the other sides are not shown.

An **informative passage** is written to teach readers. Informative passages are almost always nonfiction. The purpose of an informative passage is to share information in the clearest way. In an informative passage, you may have a thesis statement (i.e., an argument on the topic of a passage that is explained by proof). A thesis statement is a sentence that normally comes at end of the first paragraph. Authors of informative passages are likely to put more importance on being clear. Informative passages do not normally appeal to the feelings. They often contain facts and figures. Informative passages almost never include the opinion of the author. However, you should know that there can be a bias in the facts. Sometimes, a persuasive passage can be like an informative passage. This is true when authors give their ideas as if they were facts.

Entertainment passages describe real or imagined people, places, and events. Entertainment passages are often stories or poems. So, figurative language is a common part of these passages. Often, an entertainment passage appeals to the imagination and feelings. Authors may persuade or inform in an entertainment passage. Or, an entertainment passage may cause readers to think differently about a subject.

When authors want to **share feelings,** they may use strong language. Authors may share feelings about a moment of great pain or happiness. Other times, authors will try to persuade readers by sharing feelings. Some phrases like *I felt* and *I sense* hint that the author is sharing feelings. Authors may share a story of deep pain or great joy. You must not be influenced by these stories. You need to keep some distance to judge the author's argument.

Almost all writing is descriptive. In one way or another, authors try to describe events, ideas, or people. Some texts are concerned only with **description**. A descriptive passage focuses on a single subject and seeks to explain the subject clearly. Descriptive passages contain many adjectives and adverbs (i.e., words that give a complete picture for you to imagine). Normally, a descriptive passage is informative. Yet, the passage may be persuasive or entertaining.

Writing Devices

Authors will use different writing devices to make their message clear for readers. One of those devices is comparison and contrast. As mentioned above, when authors show how two things are alike, they are **comparing** them. When authors describe how two things are different, they are **contrasting** them. The compare and contrast passage is a common part of nonfiction. Comparisons are known by certain words or phrases: *both*, *same*, *like*, *too*, and *as well*. Contrasts may have words or phrases like *but*, *however*, *on the other hand*, *instead*, and *yet*. Of course, comparisons and contrasts may be understood without using those words or phrases. A single sentence may compare and contrast. Think about the sentence *Brian and Sheila love ice cream, but Brian loves vanilla and Sheila loves strawberry*. In one sentence, the author has described both a similarity (love of ice cream) and a difference (favorite flavor).

Another regular writing device is **cause and effect**. A cause is an act or event that makes something happen. An effect is what results from the cause. A cause and effect relationship is not always easy to find. So, there are some words and phrases that show causes: *since*, *because*, and *due to*. Words and phrases that show effects include *consequently, therefore, this lead(s) to, as a result*. For example, *Because the sky was clear, Ron did not bring an umbrella*. The cause is the clear sky, and the effect is that Ron did not bring an umbrella. Readers may find that the cause and effect relationship is not clear. For example, *He was late and missed the meeting*. This does not have any words that show cause or effect. Yet, the sentence still has a cause (e.g., he was late) and an effect (e.g., he missed the meeting).

Remember the chance for a single cause to have many effects. (e.g., *Single cause*: Because you left your homework on the table, your dog eats the homework. *Many effects*: (1) As a result, you fail your homework. (2) Your parents do not let you see your friends. (3) You miss out on the new movie. (4) You miss holding the hand of an important person.)

Also, a **single effect** can have many causes. For example, a single-effect sentence is: *Alan has a fever*. This fever can have multiple causes: 1) An unexpected cold front came through the area. (2) Alan forgot to take his multi-vitamin.

An effect can also become the cause of another effect. This is known as a **cause and effect chain**. For example: *As a result of her hatred for not doing work, Lynn got ready for her exam*. This led to her passing her test with high marks. Hence, her resume was accepted, and her application was also accepted.

Often, authors use analogies to add meaning to their passages. An **analogy** is a comparison of two things. The words in the analogy are connected by a relationship. Look at this analogy: *moo is to cow as quack is to duck*. This analogy compares the sound that a cow makes with the sound that a duck makes. What could you do if the word *quack* was not given? Well, you could finish the analogy if you know the connection between *moo* and *cow*. Relationships for analogies include synonyms, antonyms, part to whole, definition, and actor to action.

Point of view has an important influence on a passage. A passage's point of view is how the author or a character sees or thinks about things. A point of view influences the events of a passage, the meetings among characters, and the ending to the story. For example, two characters watch a child ride a bike. Character one watches outside. Character two watches from inside a house. Both see the same event, yet they are around different noises, sights, and smells. Character one may see different things that happen outside that character two cannot see from inside. Also, point of view can be influenced by past events and beliefs. For example, if character one loves bikes, then she will remember how proud she is of the child. If character two is afraid of riding bikes, then he may not remember the event or may fear for the child's safety.

In fiction, the two main points of view are **first person** and **third person**. The *narrator* is the person who tells a story's events. The *protagonist* is the main character of a story. If the narrator is the protagonist in a story, then the story is written in first-person. In first person, the author writes from the view of *I*. Third-person point of view is the most common among stories. With third person, authors refer to each character by using *he* or *she* and the narrator is not involved in the story. In third-person omniscient, the narrator is not a character in the story and tells the story of all of the characters at the same time.

Review Video: Point of View
Visit mometrix.com/academy and enter code: 383336

Transitional words and phrases are devices that guide readers through a passage. You may know the common transitions, though you may not have thought about how they are used. Some transitional phrases (*after, before, during, in the middle of*) give information about time. Some hint that an example is about to be given (*for example, in fact, for instance*). Writers use transitions to compare (*also, likewise*) and contrast (*however, but, yet*). Transitional words and phrases can point to addition (*and, also, furthermore, moreover*) and understood relationships (*if, then, therefore, as a result, since*). Finally, transitional words and phrases can separate the chronological steps (*first, second, last*).

Review Video: Transition Words
Visit mometrix.com/academy and enter code: 707563

Understanding a Passage

One of the most important skills in reading comprehension is finding **topics** and **main ideas.** There is a small difference between these two. The topic is the *subject* of a passage (what the passage is all about). The main idea is the most important *argument* being made by the author. The topic is shared in a few words while the main idea needs a full sentence to be understood. As an example, a short passage might have the topic of penguins, and the main idea could be written as *Penguins are different from other birds in many ways.*

In most nonfiction writing, the topic and the main idea will be stated clearly. Sometimes, they will come in a sentence at the very beginning or end of the passage. When you want to know the topic, you frequently find it in the first sentence of each paragraph. A body paragraph's first sentence is often--but not always--the topic sentence. The topic sentence gives you a summary of the ideas in the paragraph. You may find that the topic or main idea is not given clearly. So, you must read every sentence of the passage. Then, try to come up with an overall idea from each sentence.

Note: A thesis statement is not the same as the main idea. The main idea gives a brief, general summary of a text. The thesis statement gives a clear idea on an issue that is backed up with evidence.

Review Video: Topics and Main Ideas
Visit mometrix.com/academy and enter code: 407801

Passage Structure for Non-Narrative Passages

Title

Centered on the page, the title's main words are capitalized (articles, prepositions, and infinitives are not capitalized in a title). The title may have quotation marks, or it may be underlined or italicized. The title has a few words that hint at the subject of the paper and catch the reader's interest.

Introduction

An introduction summarizes the passage and the thesis statement. The purpose of the introduction is to grab the reader's attention. To do this, authors may use a quote, question, or strong opinion. Some authors choose to use an interesting description or puzzling statement. Also, authors use the introduction to explain their reason for writing.

Body Paragraph

Following the introduction, body paragraphs are used to explain the thesis statement. A body paragraph has a topic sentence, typically the first sentence. In these paragraphs, there is evidence that helps the argument of the paragraph. Also, the author may give commentary on the evidence. Be careful because this commentary can be filled with bias.

The topic sentence gives the paragraph's subject and the main idea. The rest of the body paragraph should be linked to the topic sentence. Again, the topic sentence should be supported with facts, details, and examples.

The topic sentence is general and covers the ideas in a body paragraph. Sometimes, the topic sentence may be implied (i.e., the sentence is not stated directly by the author). Also, the topic sentence shows the connections among the supporting details.

Conclusion

The conclusion should provide a summary on the passage. New material is not given in the conclusion. The conclusion is the final paragraph that may have a call to action (something the writer wants readers to do) or a question for the reader to think about.

The main idea is the umbrella argument of a passage. So, **supporting details** back up the main idea. To show that a main idea is correct, authors add details that prove their idea. All passages contain details. However, they are referred to as supporting details when they help an argument in the passage. Supporting details are found in informative and persuasive texts. Sometimes they will come with terms like *for example* or *for instance*. Or, they will be numbered with terms like *first, second*, and *last*. You should think about how the author's supporting details back up his or her main idea. Supporting details can be correct, yet they may help the author's main idea. Sometimes supporting details can seem helpful. However, they may be useless when they are based on opinions.

> **Review Video: Supporting Details**
> Visit mometrix.com/academy and enter code: 396297

An example of a main idea is: *Giraffes live in the Serengeti of Africa.* A supporting detail about giraffes could be: *A giraffe in the Serengeti benefits from a long neck by reaching twigs and leaves on tall trees.* The main idea gives the general idea that the text is about giraffes. The supporting detail gives a clear fact about how the giraffes eat.

A **theme** is an issue, an idea, or a question raised by a passage. For example, a theme of *Cinderella* is determination as Cinderella serves her stepsisters and stepmother. Passages may have many themes, so be careful to find only themes that you are asked to find. One common mark of themes is that they give more questions than answers. Authors try to push readers to consider themes in other ways. You can find themes by asking about the general problems that the passage is addressing. A good way to find a theme is to begin reading with a question in mind (e.g., How does this passage use the theme of love?) and to look for answers to that question.

> **Review Video: Themes in Literature**
> Visit mometrix.com/academy and enter code: 732074

Evaluating a Passage

When you read informational passages, you need to make a conclusion from the author's writing. You can **identify a logical conclusion** (i.e., find a conclusion that makes sense) to know whether you agree or disagree with an author. Coming to this conclusion is like making an inference. You combine the information from the passage with what you already know. From the passage's information and your knowledge, you can come to a conclusion that makes sense. One way to have a conclusion that makes sense is to take notes of all the author's points. When the notes are organized, they may point to the logical conclusion. Another way to reach conclusions is to ask if the author's passage raises any helpful questions. Sometimes you will be able to draw many conclusions from a passage. Yet, some of these may be conclusions that were never imagined by the author. Therefore, find reasons in the passage for the conclusions that you make.

Review Video: How to Support a Conclusion
Visit mometrix.com/academy and enter code: 281653

Text evidence is the information that supports a main argument or minor argument. This evidence, or proof, can lead you to a conclusion. Information used as text evidence is clear, descriptive, and full of facts. Supporting details give evidence to back up an argument.

For example, a passage may state that winter occurs during opposite months in the Northern hemisphere (north of the equator) and Southern hemisphere (south of the equator). Text evidence for this claim may include a list of countries where winter occurs in opposite months. Also, you may be given reasons that winter occurs at different times of the year in these hemispheres (such as the tilt of the earth as it rotates around the sun).

Review Video: Textual Evidence
Visit mometrix.com/academy and enter code: 486236

A text is **credible**, or believable, when the author is knowledgeable and fair. The author's motivations for writing the passage have an important part in knowing the credibility of the passage. For example, passages written about a professional soccer game by a sports reporter and one written by an average fan will have different levels of credibility.

Review Video: Author Credibility
Visit mometrix.com/academy and enter code: 827257

A reader should always draw **conclusions** from passages. Sometimes conclusions are implied (i.e., information that is assumed) from written information. Other times the information is **stated directly** within the passage. You should try to draw conclusions from information stated in a passage. Furthermore, you should always read through the entire passage before drawing conclusions. Readers often expect the author's conclusions at the beginning or the end of the passage. However, many texts do not follow this format.

Implications are things that the author does not say directly, but you can assume from what the author does say. For example: *I stepped outside and opened my umbrella. By the time I got to work, the cuffs of my pants were soaked.* The author never says that it is raining. However, you can conclude that this information is implied. Conclusions from implications must be well supported by the passage. To draw a conclusion, you should have many pieces of proof. If you have only one piece of evidence, then you need to be sure that there is no other possible explanation than your conclusion. Practice drawing conclusions from implications in real life events to improve your skills.

Outlining the information in a passage should be a familiar skill to readers. A good outline will show the pattern of the passage and lead to better conclusions. A common outline lists the main ideas of the passage in the order that they come. Then, beneath each main idea, you can list the minor ideas and details. An outline does not need to include every detail from the passage. However, the outline should show everything that is important to the argument.

Another helpful tool is **summarizing** information. This process is similar to creating an outline. First, a summary should define the main idea of the passage. The summary should have the most important supporting details or arguments. Summaries can be unclear or wrong because they do not stay true to the information in the passage. A helpful summary should have the same message as the passage.

Ideas from a passage can be organized using **graphic organizers**. A graphic organizer reduces information to a few key points. A graphic organizer like a timeline may have an event listed for each date on the timeline. However, an outline may have an event listed under a key point that happens in the passage.

Make a graphic organizer that works best for you. Whatever helps you remember information from a passage is what you need to use. A spider-map is another example. This map takes a main idea from the story and places it in a bubble. From one main idea bubble, you put supporting points that connect to the main idea. A Venn diagram groups information as separate or connected with some overlap.

Review Video: Graphic Organizers
Visit mometrix.com/academy and enter code: 665513

Paraphrasing is another method that you can use to understand a passage. To paraphrase, you put what you have read into your own words. Or, you can *translate* what the author shared into your words by including as many details as you can.

Responding to a Passage

One part of being a good reader is making predictions. A **prediction** is a guess about what will happen next. Readers make predictions from what they have read and what they already know. For example: *Staring at the computer screen in shock, Kim reached for the glass of water.* The sentence leaves you to think that she is not looking at the glass. So, you may guess that Kim is going to knock over the glass. Yet in the next sentence you may read that Kim does not knock over the glass. As you have more information, be ready for your predictions to change.

Review Video: Predictive Reading
Visit mometrix.com/academy and enter code: 437248

Test-taking tip: To respond to questions that ask about predictions, your answer should come from the passage.

You will be asked to understand text that gives ideas without stating them directly. An **inference** is something that is implied but not stated directly by the author. For example: *After the final out of the inning, the fans were filled with joy and rushed the field.* From this sentence, you can infer that the fans were watching baseball and their team won. You should not use information outside of the passage before making inferences. As you practice making inferences, you will find that they need all of your attention.

Review Video: Inference
Visit mometrix.com/academy and enter code: 379203

Test-taking tip: When asked about inferences, look for **context clues**. Context is what surrounds the words and sentences, adding explanation or information to an unknown piece. An answer can be *true* but not *correct*. The context clues will help you find the answer that is best. When asked for the implied meaning of a statement, you should locate the statement first. Then, read the context around the statement. Finally, look for an answer with a similar phrase.

For your exam, you must be able to find a text's **sequence** (i.e., the order that things happen). When the sequence is very important to the author, the passage comes with signal words: *first, then, next,* and *last*. However, a sequence can be implied. For example, *He walked through the garden and gave water and fertilizer to the plants*. Clearly, the man did not walk through the garden at the beginning. First, he found water. Then, he collected fertilizer. Next, he walked through the garden. Finally, he gave water and fertilizer to the plants. Passages do not always come in a clear sequence. Sometimes they begin at the end. Or, they can begin halfway through and then start over at the beginning. You can strengthen your understanding of the passage by taking notes to understand the sequence.

Dual passages, or comparative essays, give two passages from authors with different points of view. The format of the two passages will change with each exam. For example, the author of the first passage may give an idea from his or her point of view. The author of the second passage gives an argument against the first passage. Other dual passages will give a topic in the first passage. Then the second passage will help or provide explanation to the topic in the first passage.

You may see that the questions ask about passage one, passage two, and both passages. No matter the length or kind of passages, you should read them in order (read Passage 1 first, then move on to Passage 2). However, if your time is limited, you can read passage 1 first and answer all of the questions for passage 1. Then, read passage 2 and answer the remaining questions.

Building a Vocabulary

Learning the basics of language is helpful in understanding what you read. **Structural analysis** means to break a word into pieces to find its definition. Parts of a word include prefixes, suffixes, and root words. Knowing the meanings of these parts can help you understand the definition of a difficult word.

The main part of a word is known as the root. Prefixes are common letter combinations at the beginning of words. Suffixes are common letter combinations at the ends of words. In pieces, a word looks like this: prefix + root word + suffix. First, look at the individual definitions of the root word, prefix, and/or suffix. Then, see how they add to the root. You can use knowledge of a prefix's and/or suffix's definition to determine a close definition of the word. For example, if you don't know the definition of *uninspired* you may be able to figure it out because you know that *un-* means 'not.' Thus, the full word means *not inspired.* Learning the common prefixes and suffixes can help you define difficult words.

Review Video: Determining Word Meanings
Visit mometrix.com/academy and enter code: 894894

Below is a list of common prefixes and their meanings:

PREFIXES FOR NUMBERS

Prefix	Definition	Examples
Bi-	Two	bisect, biennial, bicycle
Mono-	One, single	monogamy, monologue, monopoly
Poly-	Many	polymorphous, polygamous, polygon
Semi-	Half, partly	semicircle, semicolon, semiannually
Uni-	one	uniform, unity, unanimous
a-	in, on, of, up, to	abed, afoot
ab-	from, away, off	abdicate, abjure
ad-	to, toward	advance, adventure
ante-	before, previous	antecedent, antedate
anti-	against, opposing	antipathy, antidote
cata-	down, away, thorou	catastrophe, cataclysm
circum-	around	circumspect, circumference
com-	with, together, very	commotion, complicate
contra-	against, opposing	contradict, contravene
de-	from	depart
dia-	through, across, apa	diameter, diagnose
dis-	away, off, down, not	dissent, disappear
epi-	upon	epilogue
ex-	out	extract, excerpt
hypo-	under, beneath	hypodermic, hypothesis
inter-	among, between	intercede, interrupt
intra-	within	intramural, intrastate
ob-	against, opposing	objection
per-	through	perceive, permit
peri-	around	periscope, perimeter
post-	after, following	postpone, postscript
pre-	before, previous	prevent, preclude
pro-	forward, in place of	propel, pronoun
retro-	back, backward	retrospect, retrograde
sub-	under, beneath	subjugate, substitute
super-	above, extra	supersede, supernumerar
trans-	across, beyond, ove	transact, transport
ultra-	beyond, excessively	ultramodern, ultrasonic

Prefixes for Time, Direction, and Space

Prefix	Definition	Examples
a-	in, on, of, up, to	abed, afoot
ab-	from, away, off	abdicate, abjure
ad-	to, toward	advance, adventure
ante-	before, previous	antecedent, antedate
anti-	against, opposing	antipathy, antidote
cata-	down, away, thorou	catastrophe, cataclysm
circum	around	circumspect, circumferen
com-	with, together, very	commotion, complicate
contra-	against, opposing	contradict, contravene
de-	from	depart
dia-	through, across, apa	diameter, diagnose
dis-	away, off, down, not	dissent, disappear
epi-	upon	epilogue
ex-	out	extract, excerpt
hypo-	under, beneath	hypodermic, hypothesis
inter-	among, between	intercede, interrupt
intra-	within	intramural, intrastate
ob-	against, opposing	objection
per-	through	perceive, permit
peri-	around	periscope, perimeter
post-	after, following	postpone, postscript
pre-	before, previous	prevent, preclude
pro-	forward, in place of	propel, pronoun
retro-	back, backward	retrospect, retrograde
sub-	under, beneath	subjugate, substitute
super-	above, extra	supersede, supernumera
trans-	across, beyond, over	transact, transport
ultra-	beyond, excessively	ultramodern, ultrasonic

NEGATIVE PREFIXES

Prefix	Definition	Examples
a-	without, lacking	atheist, agnostic
in-	not, opposing	incapable, ineligible
non-	not	nonentity, nonsense
un-	not, reverse of	unhappy, unlock

EXTRA PREFIXES

Prefix	Definition	Examples
belli-	war, warlike	bellicose
bene-	well, good	benefit, benefactor
equi-	equal	equivalent, equilibrium
for-	away, off, from	forget, forswear
fore-	previous	foretell, forefathers
homo-	same, equal	homogenized, homonym
hyper-	excessive, over	hypercritical, hypertension
in-	in, into	intrude, invade
magn-	large	magnitude, magnify
mal-	bad, poorly, not	malfunction, malpractice
mis-	bad, poorly, not	misspell, misfire
mor-	death	mortality, mortuary
neo-	new	Neolithic, neoconservative
omni-	all, everywhere	omniscient, omnivore
ortho-	right, straight	orthogonal, orthodox
over-	above	overbearing, oversight
pan-	all, entire	panorama, pandemonium
para-	beside, beyond	parallel, paradox
phil-	love, like	philosophy, philanthropic
prim-	first, early	primitive, primary
re-	backward, again	revoke, recur
sym-	with, together	sympathy, symphony
vis-	to see	visage, visible

Below is a list of common suffixes and their meanings:

Adjective Suffixes

Suffix	Definition	Examples
-able (-ible)	capable of being	toler*able*, ed*ible*
-esque	in the style of, like	picturesque, grotesque
-ful	filled with, marked by	thankful, zestful
-ific	make, cause	terrific, beatific
-ish	suggesting, like	churlish, childish
-less	lacking, without	hopeless, countless
-ous	marked by, given to	religious, riotous

Noun Suffixes

Suffix	Definition	Examples
-acy	state, condition	accuracy, privacy
-ance	act, condition, fact	acceptance, vigilance
-ard	one that does excessively	drunkard, sluggard
-ation	action, state, result	occupation, starvation
-dom	state, rank, condition	serfdom, wisdom
-er (-or)	office, action	teach*er*, elevat*or*, hon*or*
-ess	feminine	waitress, duchess
-hood	state, condition	manhood, statehood
-ion	action, result, state	union, fusion
-ism	act, manner, doctrine	barbarism, socialism
-ist	worker, follower	monopolist, socialist
-ity (-ty)	state, quality, condition	acid*ity*, civil*ity*, twen*ty*
-ment	result, action	Refreshment
-ness	quality, state	greatness, tallness
-ship	position	internship, statesmanship
-sion (-tion)	state, result	revi*sion*, expedi*tion*
-th	act, state, quality	warmth, width
-tude	quality, state, result	magnitude, fortitude

Verb Suffixes

Suffix	Definition	Examples
-ate	having, showing	separate, desolate
-en	cause to be, become	deepen, strengthen
-fy	make, cause to have	glorify, fortify
-ize	cause to be, treat with	sterilize, mechanize

There is more to a word than its dictionary definition. The **denotative** meaning of a word is the actual meaning found in a dictionary. For example, a house and a home are places where people live. The **connotative meaning** is what comes to mind when you think of a word. For example, a house may be a simple, solid building. Yet, a home may be a comfortable, welcoming place where a family lives. Most non-fiction is fact-based with no use of figurative language. So, you can assume that the writer will use denotative meanings. In fiction, drama, and poetry, the author may use the connotative meaning. Use context clues to know if the author is using the denotative or connotative meaning of a word.

Review Video: Connotation and Denotation
Visit mometrix.com/academy and enter code: 310092

Readers of all levels will find new words in passages. The best way to define a word in **context** is to think about the words that are around the unknown word. For example, nouns that you don't know may be followed by examples that give a definition. Think about this example: *Dave arrived at the party in hilarious garb: a leopard-print shirt, buckskin pants, and tennis shoes.* If you didn't know the meaning of garb, you could read the examples (i.e., a leopard-print shirt, buckskin pants, and tennis shoes) and know that *garb* means *clothing*. Examples will not always be this clear. Try another example: *Parsley, lemon, and flowers were just a few of the items he used as garnishes.* The word *garnishes* is explained by parsley, lemon, and flowers. From this one sentence, you may know that the items are used for decoration. Are they decorating a food plate or an ice table with meat? You would need the other sentences in the paragraph to know for sure.

Review Video: Reading Comprehension: Using Context Clues
Visit mometrix.com/academy and enter code: 613660

Also, you can use contrasts to define an unfamiliar word in context. In many sentences, authors will not describe the unfamiliar word directly. Instead, they will describe the opposite of the unfamiliar word. So, you are given some information that will bring you closer to defining the word. For example: *Despite his intelligence, Hector's bad posture made him look obtuse. Despite* means that Hector's posture is at odds with his intelligence. The author explains that Hector's posture does not prove his intelligence. So, *obtuse* must mean *unintelligent*. Another example: *Even with the horrible weather, we were beatific about our trip to Alaska*. The weather is described as *horrible*. So, *beatific* must mean something positive.

Sometimes, there will be very few context clues to help you define an unknown word. When this happens, **substitution** is a helpful tool. First, try to think of some synonyms for the words. Then, use those synonyms in place of the unknown words. If the passage makes sense, then the substitution has given some information about the unknown word. For example: *Frank's admonition rang in her ears as she climbed the mountain.* If you don't know the definition of *admonition*, try some substitutions: *vow*, *promise*, *advice*, *complaint*, or *compliment*. These words hint that an *admonition* is some sort of message. Once in a while substitution can get you a precise definition.

Usually you can define an unfamiliar word by looking at the descriptive words in the context. For example: *Fred dragged the recalcitrant boy, kicking and screaming, up the stairs.* The words *dragged*, *kicking*, and *screaming* all hint that the boy hates going up the stairs. So, you may deduce that *recalcitrant* means something like unwilling or protesting. In this example, an unfamiliar adjective was identified. Contrasts do not always give detailed information about the unknown word. However, they do give you some clues to understand it.

Description is used more to define an unfamiliar noun than unfamiliar adjectives. For example: *Don's wrinkled frown and constantly shaking fist labeled him as a curmudgeon*. Don is described as having a *wrinkled frown* and *constantly shaking fist*. This hints that a *curmudgeon* must be a grumpy, old man.

Many words have more than one **definition**. So you may not know how the word is being used in a sentence. For example, the verb *cleave* can mean *join* or *separate*. When you see this word, you need to pick the definition that makes the most sense. For example: *The birds cleaved together as they flew from the oak tree.* The use of the word *together* hints that *cleave* is being used to mean *join*. Another example: *Hermione's knife cleaved the bread cleanly*. A knife cannot join bread together. So, the word must hint at separation. Learning the purpose of a word with many meanings needs the same tricks as defining an unknown word. Look for context clues and try substituting words.

To learn more from a passage, you need to understand how words connect to each other. This is done with understanding **synonyms** (e.g., words that mean the same thing) and **antonyms** (e.g., the opposite meaning of a word). For example, *dry* and *arid* are synonyms. However, *dry* and *wet* are antonyms. There are pairs of words in English that can be called synonyms, yet they have somewhat different definitions. For example, *friendly* and *collegial* can be used to describe a warm, close relationship. So, you would be correct to call them synonyms. However, *collegial* (linked to *colleague*) is used for professional or academic relationships. *Friendly* is not linked to professional or academic relationships.

Words should not be called synonyms when their differences are too great. For example, *hot* and *warm* are not synonyms because their meanings are too different. How do you know when two words are synonyms? First, try to replace one word for the other word. Then, be sure that the meaning of the sentence has not changed. Replacing *warm* for *hot* in a sentence gives a different meaning. *Warm* and *hot* may seem close in meaning. Yet *warm* means that the temperature is normal, while *hot* means that the temperature is very high.

Antonyms are words with opposite meanings. *Light* and *dark*, *up* and *down*, *right* and *left*, *good* and *bad* are sets of antonyms. However, there is a difference between antonyms and pairs of words that are different. *Black* and *gray* are not antonyms, because *black* is not the opposite of *gray*. On the other hand, *black* and *white* are antonyms. Not every word has an antonym. For example, many nouns do not have an antonym. What would be the antonym of *chair*?

During your exam, the questions about antonyms are likely to be about adjectives. Remember that adjectives are words that describe a noun. Some common adjectives include *red*, *fast*, *skinny*, and *sweet*. From these four adjectives, *red* is the one that does not have an antonym.

Review Video: What are Synonyms and Antonyms?
Visit mometrix.com/academy and enter code: 105612

Listening

The Listening section of the TOEFL consists of a total of 28 questions and lasts 36 minutes. There will be 3 lectures with 6 questions each and 2 conversations with 5 questions each.

- Lectures are between 3-5 minutes each and are about university-level subject matter. Some lectures include classroom discussion between the lecturer and students.
- Conversations take place between two individuals, but also take place in an academic setting. These might include conversations between a student and a teacher, coach, or another student.

You will have a headset that will allow you to adjust the volume of the recording. Short conversations will begin with a picture to provide orientation. With longer conversations and lectures, you will be provided with several pictures and visual cues.

Tips for the Listening Section

The listening section requires you to demonstrate your ability to understand verbal information and use pragmatic understanding to interpret content, tone, and purpose.

Tip 1: Listening for Basic Comprehension

When preparing for the test, take some time to find English radio, lectures, podcasts, and videos to watch and listen to. You should pick different types of sources because during this section of the test, you will be exposed to both academic and everyday English. Practice taking mental notes of what is said and try listening for main points.

Tip 2: Listening for Pragmatic Understanding

Speakers use tone and emphasis in speech to create a certain mood or to accomplish a certain goal. After you are comfortable with listening for basic comprehension, try listening for tone and try to identify a speaker's purpose. Try also to identify whether a speaker is talking more casually or informatively and if there is a particular emotion conveyed.

Tip 3: Connecting and Synthesizing Information

As you listen to speakers talk, you will have to connect information to form conclusions. Try to notice if two speakers make opposing points or if there is a reason behind what is said. After you listen to a sample of speech, practice summarizing and restating information, then listen again to check yourself.

Listening Skills

Use the Pictures

The pictures are provided to orient you to the atmosphere and environment in which the speakers are conducting their conversation. Use those pictures as much as possible. Try to put yourself in that environment. Become one of the pictured speakers and you will be able to better appreciate the conversation and what it means.

Use Multiple Inputs

The questions will be read to you at the same time they are exposed on the screen in the form of text. Take advantage of this. Use both the visual and auditory information being presented to better understand what is being asked. Some people are better visual and some better auditory receivers of information. Since both methods of presenting questions are given, use them both to your maximum advantage.

Main Ideas

Important words and main ideas in conversation are ones that will come up again and again. Listen carefully for any word or words that come up repeatedly. What words come up in nearly every statement made? These words with high frequency are likely to be in the main idea of the conversation. For example, in a conversation about class size in the business department of a college, the term "class size" is likely to appear in nearly every statement made by either speaker in the discussion.

Voice Changes

On the TOEFL, you are expected to be able to recognize and interpret nuances of speech. Be on the alert for any changes in voice, which might register surprise, excitement, or another emotion. If a speaker is talking in a normal monotone voice and suddenly raises their voice to a high pitch, that is a huge clue that something critical is being stated. Listen for a speaker to change their voice and understand the meaning of what they are saying.

Example:

Man: Let's go to Wal-mart.

Woman: *There's a Wal-mart in this small town?*

If the woman's statement was higher pitched, indicating surprise and shock, then she probably did not expect there to be a Wal-mart in that town.

Speakers may also place stronger stress on words that are important, which helps in understanding the focal point of a sentence or can even change sentence meaning.

Example:

Man: Did *you* play baseball over the weekend?

Woman: *We* didn't play baseball. We *watched* a baseball game over the weekend.

Example:

Man: Did you play *baseball* over the weekend?

Woman: We didn't play *baseball;* we played *tennis* instead.

In these examples, the subject of the man's question changes based on which word receives the stress.

Specifics

Listen carefully for specific pieces of information. Adjectives are commonly asked about in TOEFL questions. Try to remember any main adjectives that are mentioned. Pick out adjectives such as numbers, colors, or sizes.

Example:

Man: Let's go to the store and get some apples to make the pie.

Woman: How many do we need?

Man: We'll need **five** apples to make the pie.

A typical question might be about how many apples were needed.

Interpret

As you are listening to the conversation, put yourself in the person's shoes. Think about why someone would make a statement. You'll need to do more than just regurgitate the spoken words; you must also interpret them.

Example:

Woman: I think I'm sick with the flu.

Man: Why don't you go see the campus doctor?

Sample Question: Why did the man mention the campus doctor?

Answer: The campus doctor would be able to determine if the woman had the flu.

Find the Hidden Meaning

Look for the meaning behind a statement. When a speaker answers a question with a statement that doesn't immediately seem to answer the question, the response probably contains a hidden meaning that you will need to recognize and explain.

Man: Are you going to be ready for your presentation?

Woman: I've only got half of it finished and it's taken me five hours just to do this much. There's only an hour left before the presentation is due.

At first, the woman did not seem to answer the question the man presented. She responded with a statement that only seemed loosely related. Once you look deeper, then you can find the true meaning of what she said. If it took the woman five hours to do the first half of the presentation, then it would logically take her another five hours to do the second half. Since she only has one hour until her presentation is due, she would probably NOT be ready for the presentation. So, while an answer was not immediately visible to the man's question, when you applied logic to her response, you could find the hidden meaning.

Types of Listening Problems

Types of Conversations on the TOEFL

On your test, you will encounter a variety of listening prompts which may include one or more speakers. These may include more academic or more informal speakers who may either agree or disagree with one another. You must be able to determine main ideas and viewpoints when encountering conversations.

Academic Conversations

Academic conversations are conversations on a college campus between professors, students, and other campus members. You will need to be able to summarize main ideas and recall important details.

Class Discussions

Class discussions are conversations in a classroom between professors and students. You will need to be able to summarize main ideas, but usually NOT need to recall important details.

Academic Talks

Academic talks are conversations in an orientation meeting on academic courses and procedures or where a professor might discuss a variety of college topics. You will need to be able to summarize main ideas, but usually NOT need to recall important details.

Lectures

Lectures are conversations in a classroom about academic topics. You will need to be able to summarize main ideas, and be able to answer questions such as: who, what, when, where, or why?

Active Listening

Although listening appears to be a passive process, it must be **active** in order to be effective. Indeed, the listener should have a **purpose** for listening. The precise purpose of listening need not be conscious in the mind of the listener. In general, there are four distinguished **intentions** of listening: comprehension, criticism, empathy, and appreciation. These intentions are often intermingled in the same act of listening. When we listen for comprehension, we are trying to understand the message the speaker is communicating. In order to listen for comprehension, we need to know the standards of grammar and punctuation in English. We also need to know the common forms of argument. We also need to have an understanding of the context in which the words are spoken so that we can understand the relationship between message and context.

Listening for the Purposes of Criticism

In order to listen for the purposes of criticism, one must usually also be listening for **comprehension**. It is true that in order to accurately assess the quality of a verbal communication, you will need to understand the content of the communication first. To a certain degree, however, we all apply critical listening skills to communication we have yet to fully understand. For instance, when we hear an advertisement on the radio, we know immediately that the speaker is trying to sell us something, and so we are naturally receptive or skeptical of the message, depending on our preexisting interest in the product or service. In this case, our **critical listening skills** are influencing our listening even before we have begun to comprehend the content.

Listening for Content

In almost every listening situation, the audience is required to listen for **information**. A communication can only be considered effective if the message communicates the information intended by the speaker. The **feedback** issued by the audience indicates the degree to which the information has been received accurately. When the audience is required to ask for clarification or repetition of the message, it is possible that the speaker has been ineffective in delivering his or her information. Moreover, if the audience provides no verbal feedback about a delivered message, it is possible that they either do not understand any of the message or are simply not interested in it. Of course, when there is no verbal feedback it is also possible that the audience simply understands the transmitted message perfectly and requires no clarification or elaboration.

Listening for Comprehension

There are five basic kinds of **intentional listening**: appreciative, therapeutic, discriminative, comprehensive, and critical. **Listening for comprehension** is probably the most familiar form of listening. Students in a classroom are engaged in listening for comprehension when they take notes during a lecture. Whenever we listen to an informative or persuasive speech in order to obtain information about a subject, we are engaged in listening for comprehension. The validity and accuracy of other forms of listening, such as critical listening and discriminative listening, depend on effective listening for comprehension. If an individual is unable to understand the message that is being presented, he or she will not be able to critique it insightfully.

Assessing the Characteristics of the Speaker

As part of the overall critique of a speech, an audience member should consider the personal **characteristics of the speaker**. For instance, the audience member might consider what he or she knew about the speaker before the speech, and then decide whether this information had any influence on his or her interpretation of the speaker's message. The audience member might also consider whether the speaker's personal presentation indicated credibility or made his or her message difficult to believe. Many times, a speaker with a good message and solid supporting materials comes across as vague and disorganized because of his or her physical appearance and vocal mannerisms. Audience members should try to distinguish between weaknesses in the speaker's message and weaknesses in the speaker's personal presentation.

Analyzing the Message of the Speech

When an audience member listens to a speech, he or she should be attending to three fundamental **factors**: ideas, organization, and support. The most important thing to consider is whether the speaker's main ideas are *logical and clearly expressed*. If the ideas are comprehensible, an audience member can then consider whether they have been expressed in the *logical order*, or whether the speaker has presented them in a disorganized fashion. Finally, the audience member needs to consider whether the speaker's main ideas have been adequately *supported* by argument or factual evidence. Does the speaker provide enough support for his arguments to remain credible? Is the evidence provided relevant to the main ideas of the speech?

Speaking

In the speaking section, a topic will be presented to you and you must provide a short speech in response to the topic. Both the preparation and the speech must take place within the time allowed. There is not a correct answer to the topic. You must evaluate the topic, organize your ideas, and develop them into a cohesive and coherent response.

In one of the four tasks you will have to perform will be **independent speaking** and three will involve an **integrated reading and listening** section.

You will be scored on how well you are able to utilize standard spoken English, organize and explain your thoughts, and speak clearly to address the question.

Of all the test sections on the TOEFL, this is the easiest to prepare for. This is the test section that you can practice anywhere, in your car, in your room, on the phone, by yourself, or with someone else. After you successfully pass TOEFL, you will be speaking English a lot, so you might as well prepare by speaking it at every opportunity beforehand.

Tips for the Speaking Section

The speaking section will require you to demonstrate your ability to speak English in both academic and informal settings. This involves speaking in an organized and clear manner without much preparation time. You will be asked to give four short speeches ranging from 45 to 60 seconds regarding a variety of topics.

Tip 1: Answering the Question

The speaking section of the test provides you with very little time to accomplish your goal of answering a question. Make sure that you spend your time saying things that matter and avoid saying things that do not. To practice, record yourself speaking about familiar topics. Go back and listen to yourself and identify unnecessary information. Try answering again until you think you have answered the question without digressing.

Tip 2: Speaking Clearly

A major part of speech requires you to pace yourself and speak not too quickly or too slowly. Speakers should also place adequate emphasis on key words, such as important nouns and verbs in each sentence. For practice, record yourself speaking or have someone listen to you and point out areas that are confusing.

Tip 3: Grammatical Accuracy

While speaking, grammatical accuracy plays a key point in clearly communicating what you mean. Try recording your responses to questions about familiar topics, and write down your answers or listen for grammatical errors. To help keep your grammar clear, make your points simple rather than complex.

Tip 4: Organization

Similar to the way writing should be organized with an introduction, three main points, and a conclusion, short speeches should be organized to make sure that everything that is said is to the point or supports the main objective. Practice making short arguments with clear points.

Tip 5: Using Time Effectively

Remember that the speaking section provides you with only 15-30 seconds to prepare and 45-60 seconds to answer the questions. Practice timing yourself answering questions and take note if you are speaking too quickly or including unnecessary information. Try practicing with a variety of topics.

Practice Tips:

- Make and practice a list of familiar topics and a few that you may not know much about.
- Verbally practice retelling specific days (yesterday, a holiday, etc.). Make sure to practice using prepositions and other connecting words, such as first, next, then, throughout.
- Practice telling short stories from your experiences in under a minute.
- Read or listen to a story and retell it.

Record yourself and ask yourself the following questions:

- Did I complete the task?
- Did I speak clearly?
- Did I make any grammatical errors?
- Were my points organized?
- Did I use my time well?

Preparing to Speak

Brainstorm

Spend your preparation time thinking of your main answer and a few points supporting your conclusion, as if this were a written response. Time is key, so do not try to think of too many reasons, but only what can be explained simply and clearly.

The Clear Message of a Speech

When speaking, you should be focusing on three fundamental **factors**: ideas, organization, and support. The most important thing for you to consider is whether the main ideas are *logical and clearly expressed*. If the ideas are comprehensible, you should then consider whether they have been expressed in the *logical order*, or whether you have presented them in a disorganized fashion. Finally, you need to consider whether your main ideas have been adequately *supported* by logic or facts. Do you provide enough support for your arguments to remain credible? Is the evidence provided relevant to the main ideas?

Exhausting the Possibilities

You will be prompted with some basic questions. There are only so many possible basic questions that can be asked about someone, so you can easily be prepared for every possibility. Go through and write down all the possibilities and a good answer for each. When you're asked about your family, you don't have to struggle to come up with descriptions for your family members. Practice ahead of time and know what you're going to say. Right now, as you're reading this, stop and take a minute to answer each of the following questions. If these were asked in an interview, what would you say?

1. Please describe yourself.
2. Please describe your family.
3. Please describe your home.

4. Please describe some of your interests.
5. Please describe your job.
6. Please describe your studies.

This is important practice. Make sure that you can spend a minute or so answering each of these questions without having to take time to think of a good response. These are basic questions and you should have your basic answers ready.

Tell a Story

Think about your favorite relatives. In many cases, they are your favorite because they are such raconteurs, or good storytellers. These are your aunts and uncles that can turn a simple trip to the grocery store into high adventure and keep you captivated and entertained. Even if you're not a natural storyteller, with a little thought and practice, even you can turn dull past experiences into exciting exploits.

Stories are your strongest weapon for demonstrating your mastery of speaking English. Some questions practically beg for stories to be told. These need to be compelling stories, real time drama, with you as the hero. Once you begin a quick, exciting story, you have set the tone.

The easiest way to prepare for these more difficult questions is to scour your memory for any exciting instance in your **past**, perhaps where you played a leadership role or accomplished a goal. This can be from any part of your past: during your education, at home with your family, doing a project at work, or anything that you might have had a part in. Identify the main characteristics of the story so you have the details correct. Make sure you know the basics of what happened, who was involved, why it occurred, and how the events unfolded sequentially. You certainly don't want to stumble over the facts and repeat yourself during your response.

One Size Fits All

These basic stories are building blocks. Just as a piece of lumber can be cut into many different shapes and have many completely unique uses, each of your stories does not only answer one unique question. Your stories are **one size fits all**. With practice you will find that you can use the same story to answer two seemingly unrelated questions.

For example, a question about teamwork and a question about working under pressure can both be answered by a story about your experience playing intramural basketball. The story could describe how you had to work as a team in order to get into the playoffs, spending time practicing together, coordinating plays, and whatever was necessary for the team to advance. Alternatively, the story could focus on the shots that you made that season in order to win the game in the last few seconds of play under enormous pressure. The basic story is the same: your experiences playing basketball.

The questions were different, but you **customized** the story to fit the question. With practice you should be able to answer almost any question with just a few stock stories that can be customized.

Find the Bridges

Some questions will lend themselves more readily to a story than others. You must have a set of basic stories ready that can be modified to fit the occasion. You must "find the bridges" in the questions offered to make sure your stories get told.

In WWII, the US Army used Bailey bridges. Bailey bridges were made of prefabricated steel sections that were carried around and could be thrown together at a moment's notice, allowing the army to move quickly across any obstacle and get to their destination.

You need to find bridges, i.e. **opportunities to tell your stories**. Look for any chance to turn a standard question about anything, into a bridge to begin telling your story. For example, "What is your job title?"

On the surface that might not seem like the ideal bridge, but with a little insight your response might become:

"My job title is Product Line Manager. I am responsible for everything from the development of new products to the obsolescence of old products. Marketing, sales, engineering, and production of the entire product line fall under my responsibility. One of the products was even my own idea based on feedback I received from my interactions with our customers. In the first year, it alone had achieved a sales level of over..."

The key to remember is that just because a question is **closed-ended** (yes/no or one word answers), you don't have to answer it as a closed-ended question. Answer the question asked, but then find a way to develop your answer into a bridge to a good story of yours. With an open mind, the most closed-ended of questions can become a launch pad into a story.

Practice Makes Perfect

Don't try to answer every question spontaneously. You'll spend most of your time trying to think of what happened and repeating yourself. Beforehand, think of the classic stories you could tell and then **practice** going over them with your friends, explaining how you successfully achieved the goal or took charge and gave leadership to your group project. You don't want to have the story memorized, because it will become stale in the telling, but you want it to be smooth. This story must be live and in living color, so that a potential listener could see himself taking part and watching the situation unfold. Have your friends and family members quiz you by asking you random questions and see how well you can adapt to the question and give a clear response.

Writing

You will have 29 minutes to complete two writing tasks during the writing section. The **integrated writing task** will involve reading and listening followed by a response. The **independent writing task** involves writing an argument supporting an opinion.

In each task, a topic will be presented to you and you must write out a discussion on it within the time allowed. You must evaluate the topic, organize your ideas, and develop them into a cohesive and coherent response.

These tasks will not necessarily have a right or a wrong answer. You will be scored on how well you are able to utilize standard written English, organize and explain your thoughts, and support those thoughts with reasons and examples.

Tips for the Writing Section

For the writing section of this test, you will need to answer an integrated writing task, which involves a reading or speaking comprehension section with a writing response to the topic. The Independent writing task asks you to explain and support your own opinion about an issue.

Tip 1: Integrated Writing Task

For the integrated writing task, you will need to understand and respond to written and **verbal input**. Try to take note of what is said so you can refer back to this information in your own responses for comparison or contrast.

Tip 2: Independent Writing Task

For the independent writing task, you will need to write an essay explaining and supporting your own **opinion** regarding a subject. For this, you should try to be as organized as possible, making clear points and organizing them into meaningful paragraphs. Follow the introduction, body, and conclusion format if possible. Practice discussing common issues in this format and review your work to eliminate unnecessary information. Remember that extra information only slows down and can confuse readers.

Tip 3: General Recommendations

Try to learn **descriptive adverbs and adjectives** that can be used in many arguments rather than using common words. Descriptive language can keep readers engaged and provide more detail if used correctly. Practice using a **QWERTY keyboard**, which you will need to use during this test.

The Writing Process

Brainstorm

Spend the first few minutes brainstorming ideas. Write down any ideas you might have on the topic. The purpose is to extract from the recesses of your memory any **relevant information**. In this stage, anything goes down. Write down any idea, regardless of how good or bad it may initially seem. You can use either the scratch paper provided or the word processor to quickly jot down your thoughts and ideas. The word processor is highly recommended though, particularly if you are a fast typist.

Strength Through Diversity

The best papers will contain **diversity** of examples and reasoning. As you brainstorm, consider different perspectives. Not only are there two sides to every topic, but there are also countless **perspectives** that can be considered. On any topic, different groups are impacted, with many reaching the same conclusion or position, but through vastly different paths. Try to "see" the topic through as many different eyes as you can. Look at it from every angle and vantage point. The more diverse the reasoning used, the more balanced the paper will become and the better the score will be.

Example:

The topic of free trade is not just two-sided. It impacts politicians, domestic (US) manufacturers, foreign manufacturers, the US economy, the world economy, strategic alliances, retailers, wholesalers, consumers, unions, workers, and the exchange not only of goods, but also of ideas, beliefs, and cultures. The more of these angles that you can use to approach the topic, the more solid your reasoning and the stronger your position.

Furthermore, don't just use information as to how the topic impacts other people. Draw liberally from your own **experience and observations**. Describe a personal experience that you have had and your own emotions from that moment. Anything you've seen in your community or observed in society can be expanded upon to further round out your position on the topic.

Once you have finished with your creative flow, stop and **review** it. Which idea allowed you to come up with the most supporting information? It's extremely important that you pick an angle that will allow you to have a thorough and comprehensive coverage of the topic. This is not about your personal convictions, but about writing a concise, rational discussion of an idea.

Every garden of ideas gets weeds in it. The ideas that you brainstormed are going to be random pieces of information of mixed value. Go through them methodically and pick out the ones that are the best. The best ideas are **strong points** that you can easily write a few sentences or a paragraph about.

Now that you know which ideas you are going to use and focus on, **organize** them. Put your writing points in a logical order. You have your main ideas that you will focus on, and must align them in a sequence that will flow in a smooth, sensible path from point to point, so that the reader will go smoothly from one idea to the next in a logical path. Readers must have a sense of continuity as they read your paper. You don't want a paper that rambles back and forth.

Start Your Engines

You have a logical flow of main ideas with which to start writing. Begin **expanding** on the topics in the sequence that you have set for yourself. Pace yourself. Don't spend too much time on any one of the ideas that you are expanding on. You want to have time for all of them. Make sure you watch your time. If you have twenty minutes left to write out your ideas and you have ten ideas, then you can only use two minutes per idea. It can be a daunting task to cram a lot of information down in words in a short amount of time, but if you pace yourself, you can get through it all. If you find that you are falling behind, speed up. Move through each idea more quickly, spending less time to expand upon the idea in order to catch up.

Once you finish expanding on each idea, go back to your brainstorming session up above, where you wrote out your ideas. Go ahead and scratch through the ideas as you write about them. This will let you see what you need to write about next, and also allow you to pace yourself and see what you have left to cover.

Your first paragraph should have several easily identifiable features.

- First, it should have a quick **description** or paraphrasing of the topic. Use your own words to briefly explain what the topic is about.
- Second, you should explain your **opinion** of the topic and give an explanation of why you feel that way. What is your decision or conclusion on the topic?
- Third, you should list your "writing points." What are the **main ideas** that you came up with earlier? This is your opportunity to outline the rest of your paper. Write a sentence explaining each idea that will be explained in further depth in additional paragraphs. If someone were only to read this paragraph, he or she should be able to get a good summary of the entire paper.

Each of your successive paragraphs should expand on one of the points listed in the main paragraph. Use your personal experience and knowledge to support each of your points. Everything should be backed up by **examples**.

Once you have finished expanding upon each of your main points, wrap it up. **Summarize** what you have said in a conclusion paragraph. Explain your opinion of the topic once more and quickly review why you feel that way. At this stage, you have already backed up your statements, so there is no need to do that again. All you are doing is refreshing the reader's mind on your main points.

Punctuation

If a section of text has an opening dash, parentheses, or comma at the beginning of a phrase, then you can be sure there should be a matching closing dash, parentheses, or comma at the end of the phrase. If items in a series are each separated by commas, then any additional items in that series will also need commas. Do not alternate punctuation. If a dash is at the beginning of a statement, then do not put a parenthesis at the ending of the statement.

Word Confusion

"Which" should be used to refer to things only.

John's dog, which was called Max, is large and fierce.

"That" may be used to refer to either persons or things.

Is this the only book that Louis L'Amour wrote?

Is Louis L'Amour the author that [or who] wrote Western novels?

"Who" should be used to refer to persons only.

Mozart was the composer who [or that] wrote those operas.

Pronoun Usage

To determine the correct pronoun form in a compound subject, try each subject separately with the verb, adapting the form as necessary. Your ear will tell you which form is correct.

Example: *Bob and (I, me) will be going.*

Restate the sentence twice, using each subject individually. Bob will be going. I will be going. "Me will be going" does not make sense.

When a pronoun is immediately followed by a noun (as in "we boys"), say the sentence without the added noun. Your ear will tell you the correct pronoun form.

Example: *(We/Us) boys played football last year.*

Restate the sentence twice, without the noun. We played football last year. Us played football last year. Clearly "We played football last year" makes more sense.

Using Commas

Flow

Commas break the flow of text. To test whether they are necessary, read the text to yourself and pause for a moment at each comma. If the pauses seem natural, then the commas are correct. If they are not, then the commas are not correct.

Nonessential Clauses and Phrases

A comma should be used to set off **nonessential** clauses and participial phrases from the rest of the sentence. To determine if a clause is **essential**, remove it from the sentence. If the removal of the clause would alter the meaning of the sentence, then it is essential. Otherwise, it is nonessential.

Example: *John Smith, who was a disciple of Andrew Collins, was a noted archeologist.*

In the example above, the sentence describes John Smith's fame in archeology. The fact that he was a disciple of Andrew Collins is not necessary to that meaning. Therefore, separating it from the rest of the sentence with commas is correct.

Do not use a comma if the clause or phrase is essential to the meaning of the sentence.

Example: *Anyone who appreciates obscure French poetry will enjoy reading the book.*

If the phrase "who appreciates obscure French poetry" is removed, the sentence indicates that anyone would enjoy reading the book, not just those with an appreciation for obscure French poetry. However, the sentence implies that the book's enjoyment may not be for everyone, so the phrase is essential.

Another, perhaps easier, way to determine if the clause is essential is to see if it has a comma at its beginning or end. Consistent, parallel punctuation must be used, and so if you can determine a comma exists at one side of the clause, then you can be certain that a comma should exist on the opposite side.

Independent Clauses

Use a comma before the words *and*, *but*, *or*, *nor*, *for*, or *yet* when they join independent clauses. To determine if two clauses are independent, remove the word that joins them. If each clause can stand alone as a complete sentence, then they are independent and need a comma between them.

Example: *He ran down the street, and then he ran over the bridge.*

He ran down the street. Then he ran over the bridge. Both clauses are capable of being their own sentence. Therefore, a comma must be used along with the word "and" to join the two clauses together.

If one or more of the clauses would be a fragment if left alone, then it must be joined to another clause and a comma is not needed between them.

Example: *He ran down the street and over the bridge.*

He ran down the street. Over the bridge. "Over the bridge" is a sentence fragment and cannot stand alone. No comma is necessary to join it with "He ran down the street." Note that this does not cover the use of "and" when separating items in a series, such as "red, white, and blue." In these cases a comma is not always necessary between the last two items in the series, but in general it is best to use one.

Parenthetical Expressions

Commas should separate parenthetical expressions such as the following: *after all*, *by the way*, *for example*, *in fact*, and *on the other hand*.

Example: *By the way, she is in my biology class.*

If the parenthetical expression is in the middle of the sentence, a comma is placed both before and after it.

Example: *She is, after all, in my biology class.*

However, these expressions are not always used parenthetically, so commas may not be necessary. To determine if an expression is parenthetical, see if you need to pause when you read the sentence. If you do, then it is parenthetical and needs commas.

Example: *You can tell by the way she plays the violin that she enjoys its music.*

No pause is necessary in reading that example sentence. Therefore, the phrase "by the way" does not need commas around it.

Hyphens

Hyphenate a **compound adjective** that is directly before the noun it describes.

Example 1: He was the best-known kid in the school.
Example 2: The shot came from that grass-covered hill.
Example 3: The well-drained fields were dry soon after the rain.

Use Your Ear

Read each sentence carefully, inserting the answer choices in the blanks. Don't stop at the first answer choice if you think it is right, but read them all. What may seem like the best choice at first may not be after you have had time to read all of the choices. Allow your ear to determine what **sounds right**. Often one or two answer choices can be immediately ruled out because they don't sound logical or make sense.

Contextual Clues

It bears repeating that contextual clues offer a lot of help in determining the best answer. Key words in the sentence will allow you to determine exactly which answer choice is the best replacement text.

Example:

Archeology has shown that some of the ruins of the ancient city of Babylon are approximately 500 years __________ Mesopotamian predecessors.

a. as old as any supposed
b. as old as their supposed
c. older than their supposed
d. older than a supposed

In this example, the **key word** "supposed" is used. Archaeology would either confirm that the predecessors to Babylon were more ancient or disprove that supposition. Since supposed was used, it would imply that archaeology had disproved the accepted belief, making Babylon actually older, not as old as, so either answer choice C or D is correct.

Since choice D contains the word "a," this would be correct if "predecessors" was singular. Since "predecessors" is plural (with an "s" on the end), choice C must be correct.

Furthermore, because "500 years" is used, answer choices A and B can be ruled out. Years are used to show either absolute or relative age. If two objects are as old as each other, no years are necessary to describe that relationship, and it would be sufficient to say, "The ancient city of Babylon is approximately as old as their supposed Mesopotamian predecessors," without using the term "500 years."

Simplicity Is Best

Simplicity cannot be overstated. You should never choose a longer, more complicated, or wordier replacement if a simple one will do. When a point can be made with fewer words, choose that answer. However, do not sacrifice the flow of text for simplicity. If an answer is simple, but does not make sense, then it is not correct.

Beware of **added phrases** that don't add anything of meaning, such as "to be" or "as to them." Often these added phrases will occur just before a colon, which may indicate a list of items. However, the colon does not need a lengthy introduction.

The phrases "of which [...] are" in the below examples are wordy and unnecessary. They should be removed and the colon placed directly after the words "sport" and "following".

Example 1: *There are many advantages to running as a sport, of which the top advantages are:*

Example 2: *The school supplies necessary were the following, of which a few are:*

Don't Panic

Panicking will not put down any more words on paper. Therefore, it isn't helpful. When you first see the topic, if your mind goes blank, take a deep breath. Force yourself to mechanically go through the steps listed earlier.

Secondly, don't get clock fever. It's easy to be overwhelmed when you're looking at a page that is mostly blank, your mind is full of random, confused thoughts, and the clock is ticking down faster than you would like. But you brainstormed first so you don't have to keep coming up with ideas. If you're running out of time and you have a lot of ideas you haven't covered, don't be afraid to make some cuts. Start picking the best of the remaining ideas and expand on those few. Don't feel like you have to write down and expand all of your ideas.

CHECK YOUR WORK

It is more important to have a shorter paper that is well written and well organized than a longer paper that is poorly written and poorly organized. Don't keep writing about a subject just to add words and sentences, and certainly don't start repeating yourself. Expand on the ideas that you identified in the brainstorming session and make sure that you save a few minutes at the end to review.

Leave time at the end, at least a few minutes, to go back and **check over your work**. Reread and make sure that everything you've written makes sense and flows well. Clean up any spelling or grammar mistakes that you might have made.

As you proofread, make sure there aren't any sentence fragments or run-ons. Check for sentences that are too short or too long. If the sentence is too short, check to see if you have an identifiable subject and verb. If it is too long, break it up into two separate sentences. Watch out for any "big" words you may have used. It's good to use difficult vocabulary words, but only if you are positive that you are using them correctly. Your paper has to be correct, but it doesn't have to be fancy. You're not trying to impress anyone with your vocabulary, but with your ability to develop and express ideas.

Summary

Depending on your test-taking preferences and personality, the writing will probably be your hardest or your easiest section. You are required to go through the entire process of writing a paper in a brief amount of time, which can be quite a challenge.

Focus on each of the steps listed above. Go through the process of creative flow first, generating ideas and thoughts about the topic. Then organize those ideas into a smooth, logical flow. Pick out the best ideas from your list. Decide which main idea or angle of the topic you will discuss.

Create a recognizable structure in your paper, with an introductory paragraph explaining what you have decided on and what your main points will be. Use the body paragraphs to expand on those main points and have a conclusion that wraps up the issue or topic.

Save a few moments to go back and review what you have written. Clean up any minor mistakes and give it those last few critical touches that can make a huge difference. Finally, be proud and confident of what you have written!

TOEFL Practice Test #1

Want to take this practice test in an online interactive format?
Check out the online resources page, which includes interactive practice questions and much more: **mometrix.com/resources719/toefl-28244**

Reading

Additional Instructions for the Test

When you take the real test, you will be given a university-level text. After fully reading the text, you will be able to access the questions. During this time, you will be able to refer back to the passage while answering the questions. You will have two reading passages during your test and 36 minutes to complete both passages. Take your time and remember that all of the answers can be found in the passage.

Questions 1–10 are based on the following passage.

Passage 1

(1) Although there are many disparate ideas about the definition of "plants," the most common one characterizes plants by their adaptations to land, which include the evolutionary characteristics that came about as a result of the shift out of water; these changes are especially notable when plants are compared to charophyte green algae, a group that includes land plant ancestors. These plant characteristics include a spore wall thickened by the biopolymer sporopollenin; a cuticle, which is the protective outer layer covering leaves and young shoots; an apical meristem, which is the growth at root and shoot tips; an embryonic stage with the necessary accompanying structures, which are the archegonia for eggs and antheridia for spores; and a life cycle involving the alternation of generations, meaning that there are two multicellular "phases" of plant life, the sporophyte generation and the gametophyte generation, which differ in function.

(2) To understand the plant sporic life cycle, it is necessary to understand the zygotic life cycle because plant ancestors, green algae, undergo it. The zygotic life cycle is, therefore, the precursor to the sporic life cycle, and understanding it provides a basis for comparison. The zygotic life cycle is that of algae and simple eukaryotes (organisms in which each cell contains a nucleus). The organisms that undergo this process have one copy of their genetic information in each cell, which is known as haploid. Haploid organisms can give rise only to haploid cells; accordingly, the gametes, or sex cells like egg and sperm, contain only one copy of the genetic information. The two gametes fuse in a process called fertilization, creating a diploid zygote, which is the only diploid structure in these organisms' life cycle. This zygote undergoes meiosis, a process that evenly divides the DNA into four haploid cells. Three of these cells die and one forms the haploid body of the organism. This life cycle contains only one multicellular stage: the haploid body.

(3) The sporic life cycle, however, is defined by two multicellular stages: a multicellular haploid gametophyte generation and a multicellular diploid sporophyte generation. The gametophyte stage gives rise to haploid gametes. Male gametophytes produce antheridia, which produce sperm via mitosis, while female gametophytes produce archegonia, which give rise to eggs

via mitosis. These gametes, egg and sperm, fuse to become a single-celled diploid zygote. Unlike the algal plant ancestor, this zygote then undergoes mitosis, increasing the number of cells without splitting the genetic information, and becomes the sporophyte generation, which is still diploid. The sporophyte creates haploid cells through meiosis, the dividing of the genetic information, that will eventually become the multicellular gametophyte, thus beginning the cycle anew.

(4) The relationship between the two stages of the life cycle in a single organism oscillates between dependency and equilibrium, as many organisms have a sporophyte generation that relies entirely on the gametophyte, or vice versa, while other plants have regulated into generations with more equivalency. For example, the sporophyte of mosses is dependent on the gametophyte for nutrients. Other plants, like ferns, have a large sporophyte and a much smaller independent gametophyte, and seed plants have large sporophytes and dependent, microscopic gametophytes. These generations are often morphologically distinct. The moss gametophyte in particular is recognized by its green color, and the sporophyte grows from the gametophyte on a long stem-like structure called a seta with a bulb at the top called an operculum.

(5) When considering the evolutionary process of land plants, the life cycle is a <u>crucial</u> point of discussion because all land plants descended from charophyte green algae. These algae experience the zygotic life cycle, in which the single-celled diploid zygote undergoes meiosis to create spores. In plants, however, the zygote does not immediately go through meiosis. It instead undergoes mitosis and forms a multicellular body before undergoing meiosis and creating spores. The current theory is that there was a delay in zygotic meiosis of algae that resulted in a multicellular body during the sporophyte stage. This is supported by the fact that the first lineage of land plants, the bryophytes, has a multicellular diploid sporophyte that is dependent on the multicellular haploid gametophyte.

1. According to paragraphs 2 and 3, which of the following is true about the difference between zygotic and sporic life cycles?

a. The zygotic life cycle includes a step for fertilization, but the sporic life cycle does not.
b. The zygotic life cycle's zygote undergoes meiosis immediately, but the sporic life cycle's zygote undergoes mitosis first.
c. The zygotic life cycle's gametes are haploid, but the sporic life cycle's gametes are diploid.
d. The zygotic life cycle is defined by having gametes, whereas the sporic life cycle has haploid cells.

2. According to paragraph 1, which of the following is NOT a characteristic by which plants are defined?

a. An apical meristem
b. An archegonia for eggs
c. A protective outer layer on leaves
d. A zygotic life cycle

3. Why did the author choose to include the following sentence in paragraph 5?

"In plants, however, the zygote does not immediately go through meiosis."

a. To compare the formation of the zygote in different life cycles
b. To disprove the notion that algae and plants are related
c. To suggest that plant zygotes never go through meiosis
d. To illustrate the difference between algae and plants

4. Why did the author choose to include the following sentence in paragraph 4?

"Other plants, like ferns, have a large sporophyte and a much smaller independent gametophyte, and seed plants have large sporophytes and dependent, microscopic gametophytes."

a. To give an example of a sporophyte that is not dependent on the gametophyte
b. To acknowledge the number of plants with an independent gametophyte
c. To disprove the idea that most mosses have a dependent sporophyte
d. To suggest that all modern plants have large sporophytes

5. The word *disparate* in paragraph 1 is closest in meaning to:

a. Strange
b. Noticeable
c. Clear
d. Differing

6. The word *crucial* in paragraph 5 is closest in meaning to:

a. Interesting
b. Important
c. Unique
d. Great

7. Which of the sentences below best expresses the most important information in the following sentence from paragraph 1?

"Although there are many disparate ideas about the definition of "plants," the most common one characterizes plants by their adaptations to land, which include the evolutionary characteristics that came about as a result of the shift out of water; these changes are especially notable when plants are compared to charophyte green algae, a group that includes land plant ancestors."

a. When plants moved back into the water, they underwent many changes to survive, which made them more similar to charophyte green algae.
b. Scientists cannot agree on one definition of plants, and they define plants by how similar they are to charophyte green algae.
c. Plants, which descended from charophyte green algae, are commonly defined by the modifications that allowed them to move out of the water.
d. Both plants and charophyte green algae are difficult to characterize and describe since they underwent many modifications as they shifted out of the water.

8. Which of the sentences below best expresses the most important information in the following sentence from paragraph 4?

"The relationship between the two stages of the life cycle in a single organism oscillates between dependency and equilibrium, as many organisms have a sporophyte generation that relies entirely on the gametophyte, or vice versa, while other plants have regulated into generations with more equivalency."

a. Certain plants undergo the gametophyte generation more frequently than the sporophyte generation.
b. The two generations of the sporic life cycle are either evenly balanced and independent or maintain one generation that is dependent on the other.
c. Plants have a symbiotic relationship with other organisms that is not beneficial for future generations.
d. Some plants' reproduction depends on the employment of a gametophyte and a sporophyte, which leads to a lack of equilibrium in their gametes.

9. There is a missing sentence in paragraph 2, which is reproduced below. Where would this sentence fit best?

"A diploid cell has two copies of the organism's genetic information."

To understand the plant sporic life cycle, it is necessary to understand the zygotic life cycle because plant ancestors, green algae, undergo it. The zygotic life cycle is, therefore, the precursor to the sporic life cycle, and understanding it provides a basis for comparison. [1] The zygotic life cycle is that of algae and simple eukaryotes (organisms in which each cell contains a nucleus). The organisms that undergo this process have one copy of their genetic information in each cell, which is known as haploid. [2] Haploid organisms can give rise only to haploid cells; accordingly, the gametes, or sex cells like egg and sperm, contain only one copy of the genetic information. The two gametes fuse in a process called fertilization, creating a diploid zygote, which is the only diploid structure in these organisms' life cycle. [3] This zygote undergoes meiosis, a process that evenly divides the DNA into four haploid cells. Three of these cells die and one forms the haploid body of the organism. [4] This life cycle contains only one multicellular stage: the haploid body.

a. [1]
b. [2]
c. [3]
d. [4]

10. Choose the THREE sentences below that provide an accurate single-sentence summary of a main idea of the passage.

a. The sporic life cycle is different from the zygotic life cycle because it has two multicellular stages.
b. Algae evolved from plants and developed the sporic life cycle as an adaptation when leaving their water habitat.
c. Some plants will have only sporophyte generations, and others will have only gametophyte generations.
d. The zygotic life cycle developed from the algal life cycle, which is supported by the existence of bryophytes.
e. The two generations of plants have different roles and structures depending on the type of plant.
f. Plants are defined by the adaptations they adopted as they shifted out of the water.

Questions 11–20 are based on the following passage.

Passage 2

(1) Papyrus is a native Egyptian plant that once grew abundantly along the Nile River and was used by the ancient Egyptians to make one of the earliest forms of paper, with confirmed specimens dating back to 2400 BC. Writing at this time was typically confined to business correspondence, diplomacy, and religious texts because the papermaking process was <u>arduous</u> and time-consuming. The plant had to be cut into thin pieces and placed in an overlapping pattern to create a sheet; then, the pieces were gently pressed, soaked, and pounded before a three-day soak and burnishing with a stone. Once these large sheets of papyrus were finished, they were glued to others to create long scrolls that were several meters long, and then they were stored in leather or wooden sheaths to protect them because they were quite fragile. At the time, the main form of writing was hieroglyphics, which was later replaced by the Greek or Phoenician alphabets because they were simpler writing systems. For almost four millennia, papyrus was used by the many countries surrounding Egypt.

(2) While papyrus continued to be used as paper through the 11th century AD, parchment became more prevalent in the 4th century AD. Parchment was invented in the ancient Greek city Pergamum and was made of tanned animal skin instead of plants, making it much more durable as a writing material. Parchment was used in a bibliographic form called a codex, which was composed of fascicles, or stacks of paper, bound together into a book. While there are papyrus codices from this time period, they were not common due to their <u>fragility</u>. The process of binding a codex was to place sheets of parchment on top of each other, fold them in half or fourths, and stitch them together. The stitched stacks were placed in a wooden or papyrus binding and then in another leather binding. At first, these parchment codices were filled with works by Greek and Latin writers, though the contents have largely been lost to history. By the 5th century AD, the reproduction of ancient texts was halted in favor of copying Christian religious texts due to the influence of the Catholic Church, the lack of funding for the exorbitant cost of parchment, and the one-to-three-month-long waiting period to receive a usable codex. Additionally, in the 6th and 7th centuries AD, many codices were repurposed through an intricate but destructive process called palimpsest, in which the original text was effaced so that the parchment could be used to transcribe another text in an act of superimposition. Modern researchers have developed different techniques to recover this lost information, including digital recovery and multispectral images.

(3) Parchment was used in Europe into the 15th century AD as the standard writing surface, but the role of the book changed dramatically throughout the centuries. During the reign of the

Roman Empire, the use of books spread significantly, although not to the common citizen. Researchers argue that anywhere between 10 and 15 percent of citizens in the empire could read, which is far below the nearly 80 percent of modern times but still represented an important step in literacy rates. When the Roman Empire collapsed in the 5th century AD, Germanic peoples migrated to southern Europe. This lack of interest, accompanied by violent raids, put the existence of books in jeopardy. However, many books were safely kept in monasteries, which had a longstanding tradition of preserving both holy texts and Greek manuscripts despite a preference for the former. Throughout the Middle Ages, the church and monastic institutions played an important role in maintaining and distributing information in classical and religious texts.

(4) In the 11th century AD, monastic libraries were mainly focused on religious books, and they were key in setting up networks to trade and copy books. The first mendicant (which means "beggar") orders were founded in the 13th century AD and were particularly noteworthy for their bibliographical collection of scholastic texts, maintained because their members believed in imitating Christ through absolute poverty, intellectual formation, and work. As a result, they created a hierarchy of studies that depended on libraries. Scientists, theologians, and philosophers like Thomas Aquinas and Albertus Magnus were among their ranks, and the Parisian monasteries were the heart of biblical work in the 13th century AD. Further mendicant orders were founded in the 14th century AD and continued these practices and gave rise to many bishops and cardinals. As a result, the Franciscan convent of Assisi became one of the richest monasteries after the papal library, which contained 700 volumes.

11. According to paragraphs 1 and 2, which of the following explains why parchment replaced papyrus as a writing material?

a. Parchment was less expensive than papyrus.
b. Parchment was easier to write on than papyrus.
c. Parchment was more durable than papyrus.
d. Parchment was easier to make than papyrus.

12. According to paragraph 2, which of the following does NOT explain the existence of palimpsest books?

a. There was a long wait for a usable codex.
b. The Catholic Church valued religious books more than the classics.
c. The cost of parchment was too high.
d. Bookmakers ran out of materials to make parchment.

13. Why did the author choose to include the following sentence in paragraph 3?

"Researchers argue that anywhere between 10 and 15 percent of citizens in the empire could read, which is far below the nearly 80 percent of modern times but still represented an important step in literacy rates."

a. To disprove the idea that the common Roman citizen couldn't read
b. To compare the literacy rates of the Romans and the Germanic peoples
c. To provide evidence that the Roman Empire increased the use of books
d. To illustrate how literacy rates are declining

14. Why did the author mention the names in the following sentence in paragraph 4?

"Scientists, theologians, and philosophers like Thomas Aquinas and Albertus Magnus were among their ranks, and the Parisian monasteries were the heart of biblical work in the 13th century AD."

a. To acknowledge the effort early thinkers put into their studies
b. To illustrate the long-lasting social effects of the mendicant orders' studies
c. To contrast the earlier mendicant orders with the later ones
d. To suggest that the mendicant orders were the only orders interested in libraries

15. The word *arduous* in paragraph 1 is closest in meaning to:

a. Laborious
b. Rewarding
c. Effortless
d. Strict

16. The word *fragility* in paragraph 2 is closest in meaning to:

a. Robustness
b. Roughness
c. Expensiveness
d. Delicateness

17. Which of the sentences below best expresses the most important information in the following sentence from paragraph 2?

"Additionally, in the 6th and 7th centuries AD, many codices were repurposed through an intricate but destructive process called palimpsest, in which the original text was effaced so that the parchment could be used to transcribe another text in an act of superimposition."

a. Palimpsest occurred when a codex's binding was removed and used for another.
b. Using a process called palimpsest, the author of a codex could make edits to his or her work.
c. Codices were often destroyed in the 6th and 7th centuries AD because the church did not believe in the preservation of classical texts.
d. Many old codices had their words erased so that different information could be written in their place.

18. Which of the sentences below best expresses the most important information in the following sentence from paragraph 4?

"The first mendicant (which means "beggar") orders were founded in the 13th century AD and were particularly noteworthy for their bibliographical collection of scholastic texts, maintained because their members believed in imitating Christ through absolute poverty, intellectual formation, and work."

a. The mendicant orders housed many scholarly debates among their members in the 13th century AD.
b. Due to their religious beliefs, the mendicant orders maintained an important body of academic works.
c. Given that the mendicant orders believed in following Christ's example, their members studied at the finest schools.
d. The mendicant orders were devoted to preserving the word of Christ by rewriting texts.

19. There is a missing sentence in paragraph 3, which is reproduced below. Where would this sentence fit best?

"These migrants did not have experience with reading or writing, so preserving books was not a priority."

[1] Researchers argue that anywhere between 10 and 15 percent of citizens in the empire could read, which is far below the nearly 80 percent of modern times but still represented an important step in literacy rates. [2] When the Roman Empire collapsed in the 5th century AD, Germanic peoples migrated to southern Europe. [3] This lack of interest, accompanied by violent raids, put the existence of books in jeopardy. [4] However, many books were safely kept in monasteries, which had a longstanding tradition of preserving both holy texts and Greek manuscripts despite a preference for the former.

a. [1]
b. [2]
c. [3]
d. [4]

20. Choose the THREE sentences below that provide an accurate single-sentence summary of a main idea of the passage.

a. In the Middle Ages, reproducing classical texts became less of a priority than transcribing religious texts.
b. Old systems of making writing material were uncomplicated and inexpensive.
c. Papyrus is an irrelevant material for bibliographical studies.
d. The Catholic Church was an important figure in the preservation of historical books.
e. After the collapse of the Roman Empire, an influx of people threatened the existence of books.
f. The Roman Empire was important in establishing literacy rates greater than today's rates.

Listening

Additional Instructions for the Test

There are two types of listening samples in the listening portion of the TOEFL: short lectures and conversations. There are four to six short lectures and two to three conversations, each ranging from three to five minutes long. When you take the real test, you will first see a photo that should help orient you to the material, followed by an audio clip of either a conversation or a lecture. While the audio is playing, you should take notes. Try to identify main points if possible. After listening to the audio clip, you will be given five to six multiple choice questions. **You will not be given a transcript or be allowed to listen to the recording again.** A transcript of each conversation and lecture is included for your reference after the answer explanations.

Questions 1–5 are based on the following passage.

Listening Passage 1: A conversation between a male student and a female student

Practice Audio: Listening Passage 1: Conversation
Visit mometrix.com/academy and enter Code: 407056

1. What was Claudia upset about?

a. The status of a group project for her philosophy class
b. A difficult project designing a bridge for her engineering class
c. Her difficulty in understanding Aristotle's philosophies and influences
d. Receiving a poor grade on her midterm exams

2. What were the components of the group project assignment?

a. A 20-page paper and a 10-minute presentation
b. A 20-page paper and a 20-minute presentation
c. A 10-page paper and a 10-minute presentation
d. A 10-page paper and a 20-minute presentation

3. Why does Claudia think that her group is not taking the project seriously? Select TWO answers.

a. One student does not enjoy philosophy class
b. One student did a poor job covering his material
c. Two group members have not yet started on the project
d. They know the project will not impact their grade

4. Read the following statement from the conversation and then answer the question:

Male student: *I had to carry the weight of the whole group since no one held up their end.*

What does the male student mean when he says he "had to carry the weight of the whole group"?

a. His bridge design had to hold the entire load dictated by the assignment.
b. He needed to manage everyone in his group and assign them various roles in the project.
c. He had to take on the bulk of the group work by himself.
d. He had to demonstrate how much weight the bridge could hold before it collapsed.

5. Why does the female student say: "Before this, I always loved group projects, but now my opinion has shifted"?

a. She used to enjoy group projects, but after the current negative experience, she no longer likes them.
b. She used to dislike group projects, but after the current negative experience, she now enjoys them.
c. She has changed her views of the world after learning about the ideals of notable philosophers.
d. She used to dislike philosophy class, but after this project, she now enjoys it.

Questions 6–11 are based on the following passage.

Listening Passage 2: A lecture by a male professor

Practice Audio: Listening Passage 2: Lecture
Visit mometrix.com/academy and enter Code: 517190

6. What is the main topic of the lecture?

a. The range of developmental disorders that future teachers should be aware of
b. The varied ways in which Sensory Processing Disorder presents itself
c. The cures for Sensory Processing Disorder
d. How to teach students who are interested in education and children

7. Based on the information the professor shares in the lecture, why are there sensory integration issues for someone with SPD?

a. Because people with SPD respond well to occupational therapy, or OT
b. Because the various senses of the body are interrelated and do not occur in isolation
c. Because someone with SPD is always both a sensory seeker for some senses and sensory defensive for others
d. Because Sensory Processing Disorder used to be called Sensory Integration Disorder

8. Why does the professor explain in detail about the presentation of SPD?

a. Because many of the students listening to the lecture want to become teachers and they will need to be aware of its varied presentations in students
b. Because many of the students listening to the lecture have Sensory Processing Disorder and they should learn more about it
c. Because many of the students listening to the lecture want to become doctors who will diagnose the condition and they need to understand the warning signs
d. Because SPD has a very straightforward presentation and it is easier to discuss and identify compared to other learning disabilities like ADHD

9. According to the lecture, which of the following would be considered *comorbidities*?

a. Sensory Processing Disorder and autism
b. Touch and hearing
c. Sensory Processing Disorder and Occupational Therapy
d. Occupational Therapy and classroom accommodations

10. Why does the professor not cover the specific OT interventions and classroom modifications for students with SPD in this lecture?

a. Because there are no helpful OT treatments or classroom accommodations since SPD is so varied
b. Because the students listening to the lecture aren't interested in learning about OT interventions and classroom modifications
c. Because there is no time left in the class
d. Because the textbook covers this material well and will be assigned for homework

11. According to the lecture, what are the two primary types of SPD?

a. Sensory-seeking and sensory-defensive
b. Sensory integration and sensory processing
c. The five senses and interoception
d. OT and learning disabilities

Questions 12–17 are based on the following passage.

Listening Passage 3: A lecture by a female professor

Practice Audio: Listening Passage 3: Lecture
Visit mometrix.com/academy and enter Code: 535116

12. What was the main topic addressed in the lecture?

a. The differences between Theravada and Mahayana Buddhism
b. The difference between Indian and Chinese religions
c. The different ways that meditation is used in Buddhism
d. The importance of any religion to appeal to the masses

13. According to the professor, what is the primary difference between Theravada and Mahayana Buddhism?

a. Theravada is Indian and Mahayana is Chinese.
b. Theravada was only accessible to the upper classes while Mahayana was designed to be accessible to the masses.
c. Theravada was designed after Mahayana Buddhism.
d. Theravada Buddhists were discouraged from meditating while Mahayana Buddhists stressed the importance of daily meditation.

14. What does the professor mean when she says, "We've only just started to scratch the surface here"?

a. "We are out of time today."
b. "We have covered the necessary material."
c. "We have just begun exploring this material."
d. "We have just created a little damage so the material is still usable."

15. What does the professor imply about the evolution of Buddhism in China?

a. That there is a very clear, simple, and linear path to its evolution
b. That disagreements in fundamental concepts spawned the emergence of new sects
c. That it was easily adapted from Indian culture to Chinese because of the striking similarities
d. That a consensus vote was frequently used to shape the future direction of the religion at large

16. Which TWO of the following are components of Theravada Buddhism?

a. The Four Noble Truths
b. The eightfold path
c. Increased accessibility
d. Being a "Lesser Vehicle"

17. Read the following statement from the lecture and then answer the question:

> Theravada essentially makes little effort to include those who are unable to adhere to the requirements of their religion. The Mahayana Buddhists designed their religion to appeal to a great number of people, you know, basically to be more convenient and understandable to the illiterate masses.

What does this statement imply about the number of Theravada Buddhists compared to the number of Mahayana Buddhists when these two sects were formed and today?

a. Theravada Buddhism had fewer followers than Mahayana Buddhism in the beginning, but today both have about the same number of followers.
b. Theravada Buddhism had more followers than Mahayana Buddhism in the beginning, but no longer exists while Mahayana Buddhism remains popular
c. Theravada Buddhism and Mahayana Buddhism had about the same number of followers in the beginning, but Mahayana Buddhism has more followers today.
d. Theravada Buddhism had fewer followers than Mahayana Buddhism in the beginning, and that is still true today.

Questions 18–23 are based on the following passage.

Listening Passage 4: A lecture by a male professor, with interaction from students

Practice Audio: Listening Passage 4: Lecture and Discussion
Visit mometrix.com/academy and enter Code: 843665

18. A geology student is weighing rock samples. The true weight of the rock is 12.0 grams. The student weighs it on his new scale three times and obtains the weights of 8.0 grams, 8.2 grams, and 8.1 grams. How would you describe his results?

a. Both accurate and precise
b. Neither accurate nor precise
c. Accurate but not precise
d. Precise but not accurate

19. Based on the information in the lecture and discussion, in a research study, a person's gender would be measured on what scale?

a. Nominal
b. Ordinal
c. Interval
d. Ratio

20. What does the professor mean when he says, "You hit the nail on the head"?

a. "You're working hard."
b. "You're using the right tool."
c. "Your answer is correct."
d. "Good effort, but you're wrong."

21. In what situation would the students in the class be most likely to use the information from the lecture?

a. During archery or shooting targets
b. Conducting experiments or analyzing research
c. Weighing things in a lab
d. Taking an exam in history class

22. In what way was the lecture organized to discuss the four measurement scales?

a. In order of importance
b. In cause and effect order
c. In chronological order
d. In order of increasing specificity

23. Read the following statement from the conversation and then answer the question:

Male student's response: Interval scales are essentially an intermediary between the lack of specificity of nominal and ordinal but a little less defined than ratio with no absolute zero, so I think we cannot be quite as precise as ratio but more than the lower levels of measurement.

Which of the following is the best way to paraphrase his statement?

a. Interval scale measurements are more specific and thus more precise than nominal and ordinal scales, but less precise than ratio scales because they lack an absolute zero.
b. Interval scale measurements are less specific and thus less precise than nominal and ordinal scales, but more precise than ratio scales because they lack an absolute zero.
c. Interval scales are better than ratio and ordinal scales.
d. Interval scales are the most specific and precise scales.

Questions 24–28 are based on the following passage.

Listening Passage 5: A conversation between a female professor and a male student

Practice Audio: Listening Passage 5: Conversation
Visit mometrix.com/academy and enter Code: 474952

24. What is the main problem that the student is having?

a. He wants to become a chemistry tutor.
b. He cannot find time to make it to office hours.
c. He is struggling to understand the chemistry material.
d. He does not know where the Student Resource Center is.

25. When would be the best time for Connor to meet with his professor?

a. Tuesdays and Thursdays after trigonometry class, during office hours
b. Any time the Student Resource Center is open
c. Any day besides Tuesday and Thursday because he has trigonometry class
d. Whenever his pride is in the way

26. Which TWO of the following statements about the Student Resource Center are true?

a. It is on the second floor of the library.
b. Students need a referral.
c. There are only science tutors.
d. It is free for graduate students.

27. What is meant by Connor's statement: "Availability wasn't the limiting factor; I think it was my pride."

a. I honestly felt proud about how I performed on the exam.
b. I wasn't too busy; I think I just didn't want to admit that I needed help.
c. I am not really busy but I wanted to make you proud.
d. There is a limit to how much time I can spend on this and still be proud of myself.

28. Based on the conversation, why did Connor not use the textbook to study?

a. He has not purchased it yet.
b. He was not aware that he did not understand the material.
c. He did not know that the textbook covered the material.
d. He found the writing to be dense and thought that the examples were confusing.

Speaking

Additional Instructions for the Test

When you take the real test, you will have a variety of tasks to complete for the speaking section.

In question 1, you will answer a question that requires you to respond by speaking about your own experiences, ideas, and opinions. You will have 15 seconds to prepare and 45 seconds to respond.

In questions 2-4, you will listen to information and then speak your response to a question about that topic or read and listen to information about a topic and then speak your response to a question about that topic. You will have 20-30 seconds to prepare and 60 seconds to respond.

1. Some people prefer classes that meet once a week in a single long session while others prefer courses that meet several days per week for a shorter duration. What is your opinion? Explain why.

Preparation Time: 15 seconds
Response Time: 45 seconds

2. Read the following passage and then listen to the conversation. Lastly, answer the question that follows them.

The following text was reported by the University administrators to all students and their parents. Read the announcement.

Reading passage: An announcement from university administration

The University Public Safety and Parking Services Department has decided that, effective at the start of the upcoming academic year, only juniors and seniors will be eligible to purchase campus parking permits. While there have been a limited number of available permits for underclassmen over the past few years, the Public Services department and University administration agree that reverting back to the junior- and senior-only policy is in the best interest of our campus community. This decision comes with considerable deliberation and a majority vote. It was determined that the limitation of available spaces and resultant permit fee posed a prohibitive cost for many of our students. Additionally, we believe that reserving the privilege of on-campus vehicles for just juniors and seniors will eliminate the need for the extensive application and lottery process. All interested upperclassmen will now simply register their vehicle online and pay a nominal parking permit fee. Lastly, we hope this decision will strengthen our campus community by encouraging freshmen to stay on campus and engage in any of the many wonderful campus activities and social functions offered here and eliminate the safety issues associated with alcohol consumption and driving.

Speaking Passage 1: A conversation between a male student and a female student

Practice Audio: Speaking Passage 1: Conversation
Visit mometrix.com/academy and enter Code: 161619

Question: ***The male student expresses his opinion of the University's new parking permit policy. State and explain his opinion and compare it with the University's* Public Service and Parking department's opinion.**

Preparation Time: 30 seconds
Response Time: 60 seconds

3. Read the passage from a psychology textbook and the lecture that follows it. Then, answer the question.

Theory of Mind

The theory of mind posits that humans have their own minds that they are aware of through intuition and introspection. We cannot directly see our own minds, and for this reason, the term "theory" is ascribed to the phenomenon, since the "mind" is somewhat intangible. Therefore, the word "law" cannot be applied because observations are not made with a concrete, reproducible model that can be proven after rigorous experimentation and application of the scientific method. Theory of mind allows an individual to understand via analogy, reciprocity, social interaction, and recognizing similar experiences from their own life that another person must also have a mind with desires and perspectives. When an individual demonstrates an effective theory of mind, he or she is able to understand the emotions, thoughts, motivations, and mental state of another and use this awareness to "read" and evaluate this information in such a way as to explain and predict the other person's behavior. Research indicates that humans develop the ability to understand the mental states and emotions of others through the course of normal, healthy social and cognitive development, by interacting, observing, and imitating others and by paying attention to other people and their interactions and behavior.

Speaking passage 2: A lecture by a male professor

Practice Audio: Speaking Passage 2: Lecture
Visit mometrix.com/academy and enter Code: 414825

Question: Explain theory of mind and how the professor's example illustrates the concept.

Preparation Time: 30 seconds
Response Time: 60 seconds

4. Speaking passage 3: A lecture by a female professor

Practice Audio: Speaking Passage 3: Lecture
Visit mometrix.com/academy and enter Code: 108485

Question: What are the two kinds of speciation, and how do they work?

Preparation Time: 20 seconds
Response Time: 60 seconds

Writing

Additional Instructions for the Test

On the TOEFL, you will be given two writing tasks to complete. The first task is the **integrated writing task**, in which you will read a short excerpt from a university-level text and then listen to a lecture corresponding to the text. You must then write a response to a question asking about the main ideas and how the two sources of information relate. Your response should be between 150 and 225 words, although exceeding this amount is acceptable so long as the question is answered effectively. You will have 20 minutes to write your response.

The second writing task is the **independent writing task**, which requires you to answer a question based upon your own personal experience. This may be asking if you agree or disagree with a statement and what reasons you have for thinking so. Your response for the independent writing task should be at least 100 words. You will have 10 minutes to write your response.

Integrated Writing Task

Reading passage: An excerpt from an article about social media and society

The widespread phenomenon of mass communication through cell phones and the Internet has spurred enormous controversy. Many believe that people have become less able to build bonds with friends and family members. It is impossible to deny that social media is constantly changing the way that people interact with one another. With the advent of new technologies that allow for non-simultaneous and distant interaction, people all over the world are now able to build relationships in a way that was formerly not possible. Some might say that this is a negative trend, but this new development opens up unique and effective connections.

People often feel estranged in their surroundings. There are so many hobbies and interests that people enjoy, that it can be difficult to find someone who shares the same passions. Social media is a huge benefit to these people, as they are provided with opportunities for connection to a widespread community and countless resources. Some may have always wanted to learn more about a topic without having an avenue to jump in. Social media has proven itself to be effective in educating people of all ages on a variety of subjects ranging from rollerblading to string theory.

Moreover, the Internet is especially useful for helping people find a voice. Whereas the First Amendment protects our right to free speech, many people feel that they have lost their ability to be heard. Social media allows us all to find a new way to speak confidently and ensures that every person has the opportunity to be heard.

Writing passage 1: A lecture by a male professor

Practice Audio: Writing Passage 1: Lecture
Visit mometrix.com/academy and enter Code: 395508

Question: Describe the risks discussed in the lecture and explain how they relate to the purpose of the reading passage.

Independent Writing Task

Your professor is teaching a class on environmental science and has asked a question on the class message board. Write a response to the professor's question. Your response should be at least 100 words long.

Professor: Plastic pollution has been a serious issue for decades and studies in recent years indicate that the issue is only getting worse. To combat the problem, the US Environmental Protection Agency encouraged people to reduce their consumption, reuse what they already have, and recycle everything else.

Which component of the phrase "reduce, reuse, recycle" is the most important? Why do you think that?

Avyan: The most important component of the "reduce, reuse, recycle" phrase is "reduce." Reducing consumption is the number one way that consumers can control the influx of plastic and other kinds of pollution into the environment. Take plastic water bottles for example. The best way to prevent them from ending up in the oceans, rivers, and landfills is to not buy them in the first place. This would reduce the demand and, therefore, the production of these bottles. Reusing is also a helpful tool in pollution control, but sometimes it isn't an option. Keeping with plastic water bottles, studies have shown that reusing them is not safe due to chemical leeching and the release of microplastics.

Zaynab: I think that "reuse" is the most important step in "reduce, reuse, recycle." I personally don't think that many people are willing to reduce their consumption in order to help the environment. Even though common sense tells us that reducing consumption would prevent more pollution than recycling, many people either won't compromise their lifestyles or can't afford to change their lifestyles to be more sustainable. Most food packaging is made of plastic, and it isn't the biodegradable kind. However, many low-income families are reliant on these plastic-packaged foods and don't have the money to buy different products. In this case, reusing is much more feasible. These families can reuse plastic containers for food or other storage in the home.

Answer Key and Explanations for Test #1

Reading

Passage 1

1. B: In paragraphs 2 and 3, the author states that in the zygotic life cycle, the zygote undergoes meiosis after fusion, but in the sporic life cycle, the zygote undergoes mitosis to become multicellular before meiosis. (A) Both life cycles include fertilization. (C) Both life cycles have haploid gametes. (D) Both life cycles have gametes and haploid cells.

2. D: A zygotic life cycle is the life cycle of algae and simple eukaryotes as described in paragraph 2. Plants undergo the sporic life cycle. Plants contain the structures described in choices A, B, and C; the protective outer layer in choice C is called the cuticle.

3. D: The purpose of this sentence is to illustrate the precise difference between the zygotic and sporic life cycles. (A) The formation of the zygote is not mentioned. (B) Plants and algae are related-—plants descended from charophyte green algae. (C) The author does not suggest that plant zygotes never go through meiosis; in fact, the following sentence explains that plant zygotes undergo mitosis and then meiosis.

4. A: The purpose of this sentence is to give the example of the relationship between the gametophyte and sporophyte of a fern, which is different from the relationship present in moss. It is also to give the further example of the seed plant, which similarly to the fern does not have a sporophyte that is dependent on a gametophyte. (B) The number of plants with an independent gametophyte is not mentioned, nor is the point to show that there are many or few. The point of this sentence is to provide a counterexample. (C) The sentence does not mention mosses, and most mosses do have a dependent sporophyte. (D) The author does not suggest that all modern plants have large sporophytes.

5. D: *Disparate* means contrasting or different. A clue to this is the use of *although*, which introduces a contrasting phrase. All of the other answer choices are not accepted meanings for the word *disparate* and would not make sense in the sentence.

6. B: *Crucial* means very important. A clue to this answer is that the author talks about how important life cycles are throughout the text and continues to explain life cycles in paragraph 5. All of the other answer choices are not accepted meanings for the word *crucial* and would not make sense in the sentence.

7. C: Plants descended from charophyte green algae and are defined by the adaptations they developed as they moved out of water. (A) Plants did not move back into the water. (B) The sentence does not state that plants are defined based on how similar they are to charophyte green algae. (D) The sentence does not state that plants and charophyte green algae are both difficult to define.

8. B: The gametophyte and sporophyte generations may be either balanced and independent as with ferns, or one generation can be dependent on the other as with mosses. (A) The frequency of the alternation of generations is not discussed in the passage. The word *alternation* and the description of the plant life cycle in the passage indicate that the two generations happen an equal number of times over the plant's life. However, how much time is spent in each generation and the total number of generations within a plant's life are not mentioned. (C) The author does not mention a symbiotic relationship. Instead, the author talks about the relationship between the alternation of generations found in the sporic life cycle. (D) All plants' reproduction is dependent on both the gametophyte and sporophyte generations, and there is no imbalance in gametes.

9. C: The sentence should be added in place [3] because it explains the term *diploid* after a sentence that uses the word *diploid* without defining it. This explanation would not make sense in place [1], which is between sentences about the zygotic life cycle. It might make sense to introduce the term *diploid* in place [2], right after introducing the term *haploid*, but it would disrupt the flow of information in the passage to introduce *diploid* and then go back to discussing haploid organisms. The new sentence would also not fit in place [4], which is between sentences discussing the haploid body.

10. A, E, and F: Choice A expresses the main idea of paragraphs 2-3, which differentiate the two life cycles. Choice E expresses the main idea of paragraph 4, which discusses the different forms that the sporophyte and gametophyte generation can take. Choice F expresses the main idea of paragraph 1, which defines plants by their adaptations and explains them. (B) Algae did not evolve from plants; plants evolved from algae. (C) Plants have both sporophyte and gametophyte generations. (D) The zygotic life cycle is the algal life cycle. The sporic life cycle developed from the algal life cycle.

Passage 2

11. C: Parchment was more durable than papyrus because it was made of animal skins instead of plant fibers. (A) Parchment was not less expensive than papyrus. Papyrus cost less money because it was in abundance and tanned animal skin was not. The process for making parchment was more intensive, so making it cost more. (B) The text says nothing about parchment being easier or more difficult to write on. Papyrus was described as less durable and less expensive. (D) The text does not state that parchment was easier to make. While making papyrus was not easy, parchment was probably more difficult to make because tanning animal leather required skinning an animal and soaking and stretching the skin before scraping excess tissue off and drying it.

12. D: The text does not state that bookmakers ran out of the materials to make parchment. Parchment is made of tanned animal skin, and while the process was labor intensive, there was a steady supply of it. (A) There was, however, a long wait time to receive a codex. The passage states that the wait for a usable codex could be as long as three months. (B) The Catholic Church valued religious books more than the classics, and its monasteries held many books. Whether in religious fervor or due to a need to transcribe different religious information, many classic texts were scraped away in favor of Christian religious texts. (C) The cost of parchment was too high for many libraries or monasteries to afford. The process of making parchment alone was labor intensive, so the bookmakers charged high fees.

13. C: This sentence comes directly after a sentence stating that book use during the time of the Roman Empire went up significantly. To support this point, the author uses statistics and percentages to show the reader the rates of literacy during this time period. (A) The passage states in the sentence prior to the one in the question that the common Roman citizen could not read. Only the nobles and rich families in Rome would have been able to pay for an education. Most working individuals did not have the funds or time to learn how to read. (B) The passage does not compare the literacy rates of the Romans and the Germanic peoples. Instead, it merely states that the Germanic peoples held raids that threatened books created by the Roman Empire. The passage does not mention the literacy rates because they are unknown. (D) The passage does not use this sentence to state that literacy rates are declining. In the sentence, it explains that modern-day literacy rates are high compared to those in classical times. Despite the difference, though, the author maintains that the Roman Empire represented an important surge in literacy rates.

14. B: The author mentions these names to illustrate how the beliefs held by the mendicant orders created long-lasting societal effects. Namely, these results include important thinkers like Thomas Aquinas and Albertus Magnus. These individuals were educators within the mendicant orders and had received formal education from their families. Mentioning the names of these two important theologians and philosophers, whose works are still studied today, gives more credence to the author's claims about the importance of the mendicant orders' hierarchy of studies. (A) This answer does not make sense because the author only mentions the names of important thinkers that taught within the initial mendicant orders. The author does not explain how they received their education or the difficulties they underwent. While it would have been difficult to get an education in this time period, both Aquinas and Magnus were educated before joining their orders. (C) Both Aquinas and Magnus were in the first mendicant orders founded in the 13th century AD, which does not allow for a comparison to the further orders founded in the 14th century AD. Instead, the author mentions how the first and later orders were similar by marking the continuation of practices. (D) The author does not imply that the mendicant orders were the only orders interested in libraries. He or she merely conveys that they greatly impacted the spread and preservation of knowledge through their focus on maintaining libraries.

15. A: The sentence states that the process of papermaking was arduous and time-consuming. The author then describes the difficult and lengthy procedure for making papyrus paper. The word *laborious* means requiring much energy, time, and effort, and it is the only word that makes sense in this context. (B) *Rewarding* means to give satisfaction or gratification when completing or doing a task. Because the author does not describe the workers' feelings about making papyrus paper or their pay, the reader cannot assume that the process was rewarding. (C) *Effortless* means requiring little effort, time, or energy. This word is the opposite of *laborious* and is not appropriate to describe the labor-intensive process of making papyrus paper. (D) *Strict* means having specific rules that must be observed. This word makes little sense in this context. Although the author does mention many steps in the production process, he or she does not imply that these steps included rigid, precise rules.

16. D: The word *fragility* describes something that is weak or easily broken. *Delicateness* is the only word that could be a synonym in this case as it means something easily destroyed. In the sentence, the author mentions the *fragility* of papyrus to indicate why it was used less frequently than parchment in codices. One reason was that papyrus was easily torn (broken) and parchment was more robust. In addition, paragraph 1 uses the word *fragile*, which is a form of the word *fragility*, when explaining that papyrus scrolls were kept in leather or wooden sheaths to protect them because they could be destroyed easily. (A) *Robustness* means to be in good condition and unlikely to break. In this case, papyrus paper should not be described as *robust* because it was likely to break. (B) *Roughness* would be used to describe the texture of papyrus instead of its durability. The author does not state what the texture of papyrus paper was, and the word is not an appropriate synonym for *fragility* because they have very different meanings. (C) *Expensiveness* refers to something that costs a lot of money. While expensive things can sometimes be fragile, this is not always the case. Papyrus paper may have been comparatively expensive relative to paper prices today, but *expensiveness* is not a synonym for *fragility*.

17. D: The sentence above states that in the 6th and 7th centuries AD, many codices were effaced (erased) so that new information could be transcribed. This answer states that the codices were erased so that different information could be written on the same pages. It is an appropriate restatement of the sentence because it states that codices were changed so that they could hold different information. (A) The sentence does not state that the binding, or outside cover, of the text was changed. It states that the original text itself was effaced and does not mention the binding in the process of palimpsest. (B) The sentence shows that palimpsest was an act of destruction in which the entirety of a codex was erased. It was not used for editing a text but for replacing it. (C) While the church did participate in the practice of palimpsest, this sentence does not mention the church or its involvement in palimpsest. The sentence only explains what palimpsest was and why it was done.

18. B: The mendicant orders believed in following the example of Christ, which meant to live in poverty, to work, and to learn. As a result, the orders kept collections of academic or scholastic texts that were used to teach other members of the orders. Therefore, their religious beliefs led the orders to keep their noteworthy collection of codices. (A) The author does not state that the mendicant orders led scholarly debates. Instead, the author states that the orders had large book collections that held scholastic or academic texts. (C) The sentence does not state that the members of the orders went to the finest schools, but it does state that the orders maintained an important collection of codices to help teach their members. In addition, the members of the orders lived in absolute poverty and thus could not have paid to attend the finest schools. (D) While palimpsest was common in this time period, the sentence does not state that these orders participated in effacing codices. It merely asserts that these orders had a noteworthy collection of codices for the purpose of educating their members.

19. C: The new sentence is referencing the Germanic peoples who migrated to southern Europe when the Roman Empire collapsed. The phrase *these migrants* cannot be in reference to the citizens of the Roman Empire (who were already there), so it must be in reference to the Germanic peoples. The second sentence introduces the Germanic peoples, and it provides context to the sentence that then follows. The new sentence explains the lack of interest in books and preserving them, which is necessary in space [3]. (A) The sentence would not make sense at the beginning of this section because the Germanic migrants have not yet been introduced. (B) It would not make sense to mention the migrants' lack of interest in reading before introducing them as a whole. This paragraph construction would be confusing and unclear for readers. (D) Putting the sentence in place [4] would not make sense. The second sentence introduces a new concept: the Germanic peoples who migrated to southern Europe. The third sentence talks about how their violent raids damaged books. The fourth sentence discusses how, despite the damage, the Catholic Church was able to protect many of the books. This structure would be interrupted by placing the new sentence in place [4], and it would confuse readers.

20. A, D, and E: (A) In paragraph 2, the author states that the reproduction of ancient texts was halted in favor of copying Christian texts. The author connects this idea to that of palimpsest by explaining how this change in values led to fewer classical codices and more Christian codices. (D) The author states in paragraph 2 that the Catholic Church had influence over the storage of books. In paragraph 3, the author states that the Catholic Church and its monastic institutions played an important role in maintaining and distributing classical and religious texts. Furthermore, in paragraph 4, the author details how Catholic orders were important in the preservation and distribution of books. (E) The author discusses, in paragraph 3, that after the collapse of the Roman Empire, many groups of Germanic peoples migrated to southern Europe. Their lack of interest in reading and their violent raids threatened the existence of books in European countries, but the Catholic Church was able to preserve many codices. (B) Old systems of making writing material were not uncomplicated or inexpensive. As explained in paragraphs 1 and 2, making papyrus scrolls and making parchment were labor-intensive tasks. Furthermore, parchment was very expensive—the author describes the costs as exorbitant and too high. (C) Even though papyrus was eventually replaced by parchment, it is still important for bibliographical studies because it is one of the first forms of paper to ever exist, and so book historians are interested in how it was used. (F) The Roman Empire was important in establishing literacy rates as discussed in paragraph 3; however, the author states that the literacy rates today are closer to 80 percent instead of the 10 to 15 percent seen in the Roman Empire.

Listening

1. A: At the beginning of the conversation, the female student, Claudia, informs the male student, Miguel, that she is stressed about a big project in her philosophy class. She says, "I love the material we are learning but I'm frustrated by a big assignment that's due next week." She later reveals to Miguel that it is a midterm group project. Miguel was the one who had the bridge project for engineering, so Choice B is incorrect. There is no mention of the fact that she is struggling to understand the philosophies, so Choice C is incorrect; in fact, she says she's enjoying the material. She has not yet received the grade for the midterm because the project is due on Monday, so Choice D is incorrect.

2. D: Claudia says that the group must write a 10-page paper and give a 20-minute presentation on notable philosophers.

3. B, C: Claudia says that she feels that the people in her group are not taking the project seriously. She tells Miguel, "It's due on Monday and two of the people have yet to start their sections and the other student's piece was terrible." Choice A is incorrect because there is no mention that anyone in the group doesn't enjoy the material, just that one did not cover the assigned requirements in his section. Choice D is incorrect because there is no mention that anyone in the group doesn't think the project will impact their grade. In contrast, it is mentioned that the project is worth 40% of each student's overall course grade.

4. C: When Miguel says that he "had to carry the weight of the whole group since no one held up their end" he means that he had to take on the bulk of the work. He adds, "It was so much work to do by myself." This is a figure of speech and not to be taken literally; it does not relate to the bridge supporting a certain weight before collapsing as indicated in Choices A and D. It also does not indicate that he managed the others' work, just that he did most of the work himself.

5. A: Claudia says, "Before this, I always loved group projects, but now, my opinion has shifted" to convey that she used to love group projects but now that has changed (shifted) due to the current negative experience with her group, so she no longer likes them. Choice B essentially reverses her shift. Choices C and D may be true, but her statement does not actually relate to the course material but rather to the group assignment, so they are also incorrect.

6. B: The main topic of the lecture is the varied ways in which Sensory Processing Disorder (SPD) impacts students. The professor talks about the range of symptoms of the disorder, how these symptoms play out in the classroom, and that there are various classroom accommodations that may provide assistance to a student with the disorder. Choice A is incorrect because it is never mentioned that SPD is a developmental disorder, and even if it was, the focus of the lecture is on the specific issue of SPD, not developmental disorders in general. Cures for SPD are not mentioned, so Choice C is incorrect, and while the students listening to the lecture are in an education class and likely want to become teachers, the lecture is not about how to teach them, so Choice D is incorrect as well.

7. B: The professor says that "integration issues can manifest in a variety of ways because there are several senses and the reliance on them overlaps in most situations ... it's very rare that you only see something but there is no auditory input, or that you'd taste something without also having some degree of smell input. With integration issues, sometimes it is these combinations that create issues with interpreting the signal." Essentially, sensory input among the five senses is often concurrent and interrelated, which can make the simultaneous processing and combining of these stimuli challenging for the brain of someone with SPD. The professor adds that "the impact of SPD on an individual can be far-reaching because of the number of senses and the way in which they interact in an integrated way normally, to help us make sense of our environment and our body within the environment." Choice A is incorrect because, although true, it does not answer the question posed. Choice C is incorrect because an individual with SPD may be both a sensory seeker and sensory-defensive, but this is not always (and in fact, not often) the case. While Choice D (that SPD used to be called Sensory Integration Disorder) is true and has to do with integration, it does not answer *why* someone with SPD has integration issues.

8. A: The professor explains the variety of ways that SPD may present in a person because the students he is speaking to want to become teachers and they will likely encounter students with SPD. The end of the lecture also makes it clear that there are classroom accommodations and ways that teachers can modify their instruction to help students with SPD, which again will be helpful to discuss because many of the students listening to the lecture want to become teachers. This is evidenced by the fact that the professor says, "Today, we are continuing our discussion of different developmental and neurological disorders that your future students may have."

9. A: *Comorbidities* are two or more coexisting medical or health conditions. The only answer choice that provides two conditions is Choice A, SPD and autism. In fact, these are often concurrent disorders. As the professor explains, "Sensory Processing Disorder is often accompanied by other learning disorders or behavioral and developmental issues, such as autism, ADHD, and anxiety disorders. If students have concurrent disorders, or what we refer to as comorbidities, these should be considered in conjunction when determining classroom accommodations and overall treatment." Touch and hearing (Choice B) are both senses, but are not considered comorbid conditions because they are not abnormalities.

10. D: The professor does not cover the specific OT techniques and classroom accommodations because he says that the textbook does a good job covering that material. The listening passage ends with his comment: "Your textbook does a good job covering suggested classroom accommodations for all sorts of SPD-related challenges, so let's review particular OT strategies and classroom modifications next class after your reading assignment." While the time remaining in class may be running out (Choice C), this is not the reason he cites, so it is not the correct answer.

11. A: The professor spends a great deal of time discussing the challenges of understanding and recognizing SPD because of its varied presentation, particularly in regards to the two markedly different subtypes: those who are sensory seekers and those who are sensory-defensive.

12. A: This lecture is mainly focused on the differences between Theravada and Mahayana Buddhism, which are two sects of Buddhism that divided from one another when there were disagreements about the fundamental concepts of the religion. While the fact that Chinese Buddhism took off in different directions than its Indian Buddhism roots is mentioned (Choice B), this is not the main topic of the lecture. Choice C is incorrect because meditation is mentioned, but not the different ways meditation is used. The importance of a religion appealing to the masses was not the overall topic of the lecture, making Choice D incorrect.

13. B: The lecture focuses significant attention on the fact that Theravada and Mahayana Buddhism differed from one another in the sense that for the most part Theravada was only accessible to the upper classes due to the emphasis it placed on meditation (which was not possible for the working classes because they lacked sufficient leisure time), while Mahayana was designed to be accessible to the masses by removing this requirement. Choice A is incorrect because the lecture focuses on both of these sects of Buddhism as practiced in Chinese history. Choice C is incorrect because Mahayana Buddhism split from Theravada in response to factors of Theravada Buddhism that some people disagreed with. Therefore, Theravada Buddhism preceded Mahayana Buddhism. Choice D is incorrect because it reverses the information provided in the lecture about the focus on meditation.

14. C: "We've only just started to scratch the surface here" means that the topic is just beginning to be explored. The professor says, "I know we've only just started to scratch the surface here and there is a lot of layers we'll get to uncover about these sects in the coming days, but in an effort to not overwhelm you, let's end here a bit early and pick up next class." The class will have a lot more "layers to uncover," meaning there is a lot more to learn and discover in future classes. This phrase is a figure of speech and not to be taken with a literal meaning, so Choice D is incorrect.

15. B: The professor implies that when Buddhism came to China from India, it underwent many changes because China had its own culture and language. This new context allowed the religion to be particularly "malleable," or flexible and easily changeable (so Choice C is incorrect). She further explains, "When followers of the same religion begin to disagree on fundamental issues, the religion inevitably splits to form two new interpretations of the original. Today, we are going to talk about the first of these splits, which resulted in the formation of the Mahayana and Theravada branches of Buddhism." Choice A is wrong, because it is quite clear that the religion did not have a simple, linear path of evolution, which is why the whole lecture revolves around one of the many splits that occurred over time. A consensus vote did not dictate the direction of the religion (Choice D). Splits occurred when people in the religion disagreed about fundamental concepts. A majority vote was not needed to approve a change or new sect.

16. A and B: The Four Noble Truths ("all known existence is suffering, suffering is caused by desire, one must eliminate desire to eliminate suffering, and one must follow the eightfold path in order to eliminate desire") and the eightfold path ("maintaining the Right View, Right Intention, Right Speech, Right Action, Right Livelihood, Right Effort, Right Mindfulness, and uh ... Right Concentration") are central tenets of Theravada Buddhism. Choice C is incorrect because Theravada focused a great deal on meditation, so a great deal of one's time was to be dedicated to deep mediation. This made it less accessible to "the masses" because working-class Chinese people had to work and could not dedicate so much time to unpaid meditation. While Mahayana Buddhists considered Theravada to be the "Lesser Vehicle" (Hinayana), this is not a component of the sect and therefore, Choice D is incorrect.

17. D: Mahayana Buddhism is described as being more accessible than Theravada Buddhism and that it was created to appeal to many people. While people today are more likely to be able to read than at the time that these sects were formed, it remains true that relatively few people have the time or interest needed to adhere to a strict religion that requires many hours of meditation. Mahayana Buddhism is convenient to practice and easy to understand, and so it is likely to have been more common both when it was formed and now.

18. D: This student's measurements are precise but not accurate. Recall the response from the female student that explains this concept well: "Accuracy refers to the closeness of a measured value to a standard or known value. For example, hmmm ... if you obtain a weight measurement of 3.8 kilograms for a given substance, but the actual weight is 10 kilograms, then your measurement is not accurate. Precision, on the other hand, refers to like the closeness of two or more measurements of the same item to each other. Using the same example, if you weigh a given object five times, and get 3.6 kilograms each time, then your measurement is very precise." The geology student's rock samples are very much like that example of precise but inaccurate measurements.

19. A: A person's gender is measured on the nominal scale, which is also called the categorical scale because it simply assigns values to categories without any rank or order attached to the categories. The professor also mentions this specific example at the end of the lecture when he says: "For instance, we know gender is nominal. It's generally easy to identify someone as male or female so you are less likely to make a mistake."

20. C: "You hit the nail on the head" is a phrase that means "you are right on!" or "you are correct!" Coincidentally, it can be related to the lecture material: it's like hitting the bull's-eye, being both accurate and precise.

21. B: This lecture and discussion took place in a statistics course and would be most applicable to students when they are conducting experiments or evaluate research done by other people. The professor says, "We've been looking at the hierarchy of the four scales of measurement we use in research, which will be important for you to consider as you design your own experiments and evaluate research."

22. D: The lecture discussion is structured to address the four levels of measurement scales in order of increasing specificity. This is essentially the key takeaway of the lecture. Choice A, order of importance, may be an attractive answer, but the professor never says that one level of measurement is more important than any other, just that they have different levels of specificity, accuracy, and precision. Some things have to be measured on certain scales, but the individual scales are not more important than others overall. There is no cause and effect (Choice B) or chronology (Choice C) involved in the lecture.

23. A: Something that is well-paraphrased should be shorter and simpler than the original sentence while still maintaining its accuracy and important points. Of the options provided, Choice A was the best way to paraphrase the given sentence because it accurately restates the points that the student made but in fewer words. Choice B is not an accurate paraphrase of the original sentence. Choices C and D are attractive because they are much shorter and easier to read than the original sentence, but they are also not accurate paraphrases.

24. C: The student, Connor, is having trouble understanding the chemistry material, especially balancing equations and different types of bonds. This is evident in the first several exchanges between Connor and his professor. Choice A is incorrect because he needs a chemistry tutor but does not want to become one. Choice B is incorrect because he says he can make it to office hours. Choice D is true in that Connor does not know where the Student Resource Center is, but this is not the main problem he was having. Instead, it is a secondary question that arises during the conversation about his difficulty with the chemistry material.

25. A: In response to the professor's suggestion that he come to office hours, Connor says: "I can come on Tuesdays and Thursdays after my trigonometry class." Later in the conversation, the professor confirms by saying, "I'd like you to start coming to my office hours twice a week after your trigonometry class."

26. A and B: The part of the conversation that contained this information was the professor's explanation of what the Student Resource Center is. She says, "It's a room in the library on the second floor with all of the reference materials. The University has a bunch of paid tutors who work with students in a variety of subjects. It's free for all undergraduate students because it is included in your tuition bill, and graduate students just pay a nominal fee." She follows up by adding, "There are several great tutors to cover all of the sciences, including chemistry. I will fill out a referral form for you." From this information, test takers can determine that the Student Resource Center is on the second floor of the library (Choice A) and that students need a referral (Choice B). Choice C is incorrect because there are a variety of tutors in all subjects, not just science, and Choice D is incorrect because the services are free for undergraduates but graduate students must pay a small fee.

27. B: "Availability wasn't the limiting factor; I think it was my pride" is best rephrased by the sentence: "I wasn't too busy; I think I just didn't want to admit that I needed help." The *limiting factor* refers to something that got in the way of accomplishing or doing something else. Connor says availability (or time) was not the limiting factor, so he is not "too busy." The phrase *pride gets in the way* means that a person does not want to show or reveal that he or she doesn't understand something because that would be embarrassing and would negatively impact his or her self-esteem.

28. D: Connor mentioned that he did refer to his textbook to try to review the material about chemical structure and bonding, but he found the writing dense (i.e., hard to understand and read) and the examples seemed confusing. He does have the textbook, and knows that it covers the material that he does not understand, but did not find it helpful.

Speaking

1. Sample response: I prefer when classes meet at least two or three times per week rather than just one long session. I find that it's hard for me to sit through a class that is more than an hour or so, and some courses offered by the university that only meet once a week are nearly four hours! I really struggle to maintain focus much longer than an hour and my hand gets tired from taking notes. Even if the professor gives a break, it never fully rejuvenates me. The other issue I have with classes that only meet once a week is that it is hard to remember to keep up with the work. After you get through the marathon session, you're so relieved to be done that it's easy to just dump the books in your room and before you know it, the week has rolled by and you haven't started on the work. When they meet every other day or so, you're forced to stay on top of the material better. Lastly, if you get sick and have to miss a class, if that's the one day the class meets, it's a big hassle to make up the work, and for that reason, some professors don't even allow absences without significantly penalizing your grade.

Explanation of sample response scoring: This is a very strong response that would score a 4 out of 4 on the test. The speaker began by answering the question and then provided several reasons for preferring to attend shorter classes several days per week rather than one long class once a week. There is sophisticated vocabulary such as "rejuvenates" and "marathon session." The final sentence is complex and clearly explains the problems associated with missing class when the class only meets once per week. There are no significant grammatical errors. The phrase " the professor gives a break" would be improved if it were "the professor gives us a break," but the meaning is clear and it would not impact the score for this answer.

2. Sample response: The male student, um, Adam, is unhappy about the University's decision that freshmen and sophomore students will not be allowed to purchase campus parking permits anymore. He has a car and enjoys getting off campus to see movies or shoot pool with his friends and likes being able to come and go whenever he wants instead of waiting for a bus and thinks that as long as a student can afford it, they should be able to buy the permit. On the other hand, the University, um, Parking Services department thinks that returning to the policy where only juniors and seniors can park on campus is best for the students because there aren't enough spaces for everyone to bring their cars so the permit fees are really expensive which isn't fair for students who don't have a lot of money. Um ... it also will allow all juniors and seniors who want to have their cars on campus to just register for parking instead of needing to get lucky in the lottery. The University thinks that not letting everybody bring their cars will encourage freshmen to try free campus activities sponsored by the University and prevent drunk driving.

Explanation of sample response scoring: This response would score a 3 out of 4. The speaker begins by clearly summarizes Adam's opinion and reasons for holding that opinion. The speaker then transitions to the opinion held by the University Public Safety and Parking Services department by saying "on the other hand" and referring to the name of the department. The speaker covers all of the important points made in the University's announcement and Adam's conversation with Janice, and is mostly correct in what was said; however, it is the female student who describes the free on-campus activities, while the University's announcement only mentions that there are campus activities available. Finally, the speaker did not pause between some thoughts, so the transcript shows some run-on sentences.

3. Sample response: Theory of mind is an idea that is like empathy and, um, describes the awareness and appreciation that people can have that other people also have a mind with unique thoughts, desires, and intentions. When a person develops a good theory of mind, that person can recognize another person's thoughts and feelings and also use that information and their own experiences to anticipate and rationalize the other person's intentions and behaviors. The professor's example of the woman with, um, autism he worked with in graduate school shows what happens when someone doesn't have a well-developed theory of mind. This woman had difficulty in her social interactions because she often misunderstood the feelings, knowledge, and interests of other people. For example, it was challenging for her to grasp the concept that other people may have less experience and less interest in computer games. It was hard for her to imagine that the people around her had totally different experiences, opinions, and feelings.

Explanation of sample response scoring: This response would score a 4 out of 4. The speaker clearly explains the idea of theory of mind using wording that is easier to understand than the professor's lecture. This shows that the speaker understands the lecture and the vocabulary needed to summarize it. The speaker also explains the professor's example very well, accurately describing the difficulties that the professor's coworker had with understanding that other people did not experience life the same way that she did.

4. Sample response: Speciation is when there is one species, and it is to two species. There are two: sympatric and allopatric. Allopatric, uh, speciation is when you have a species, and there is a separation that makes two groups, but the groups cannot see each other. Changes happen in the groups, and they cannot have babies anymore. Sympatric speciation happens on the same land. It does not happen to animals, but plants sometimes have a lot of extra DNA. They cannot make other plants when there is too much DNA, so the plant with too much is a new species.

Explanation of sample response scoring: This response would score a 2 out of 4. The speaker tended to use repetitive wording to explain the concepts; for example, "when there is one species, and it is to two species," which makes the speech unclear. The speaker also did not use specific language. The lecture mentions that allopatric speciation is usually due to a physical separation. While the speaker did mention a separation, the speaker did not talk about the physical nature, instead saying the groups "cannot see each other." This explanation is not as detailed as a response that would receive a higher score. The speaker also did not explain that the two groups "cannot have babies anymore" means that the two groups cannot reproduce with one another and so are now different species. The explanation of sympatric speciation was much clearer than that of allopatric speciation. While the vocabulary is not as specific as it could be, the speaker did a good job of discussing a change that could occur in organisms that occupy the same land that results in new species.

Writing

1. Sample response: The lecture discouraged social networking by discussing how social networking has many risks. First, the lecture talks about how the Internet can be used to steal or to bully people, including both adults and children. The second point is the main point, however, which explains statistics about how people trusted fewer people with important matters. This suggests that relying on the Internet is causing people to be isolated and not spend as much time with people. Overall, the lecture suggests that social networking has too many risks and is leading our culture in a bad direction.

The lecture and reading passage have opposing views about the use of social media. The reading passage listed several positive qualities of using social media, such as how it helps people learn about hobbies and meet people with the same interests. It also encouraged social media use to help people find a voice. It says that people sometimes have a hard time finding people around them with the same interests, but that through social media, they can find friends.

The lecture and the reading passage both talk about the good and bad effects of social media. The two passages agree on almost nothing except to be careful with new technology. Whereas the lecture focuses mainly on risks, the reading passage focuses on convincing the reader that the rewards outweigh the risks.

Explanation of sample response scoring: This response is very good and would score a 4 out of 4 on the test. The response is structured like a small essay, and it contains no grammatical errors. The first paragraph describes the risks of the Internet and social media as discussed in the lecture, including a summary of the main point of the lecture. The second paragraph describes the reading passage, which is about the benefits of the Internet and social media. The final paragraph compares the main ideas of each, which directly answers the question of how the reading passage and the lecture relate to tone another.

2. Sample response: In my opinion is Avyan right when he says that reduce is important. It helps reducing the number of plastic bottles in nature. He also says that reusing is not good, but Zaynab says reusing is good. When you reuse things, you spend less money and there is less. The most important component is reduce. It is important to buy less things because those things go back into the planet. When everybody does not buy, it is easier to not have in the grass or water. When people buy, they sometimes do not reuse, and the plastic is in the nature. Reuse is important, but people do not reuse it. Also, you cannot reuse forever, and you have to throw plastic away. Then, there is still plastic.

Explanation of sample response scoring: This is a mid-level response, which would probably score a 3 out of 5 on the test. While the writer does provide an argument that is distinct from the other two responses, the language is often quite unclear. The writer begins by explaining the thoughts of the other two students but does not offer much about his or her own thoughts until the second half of the response. In the second half, the writer posits that reducing is more important than reusing because even when people reuse their consumption, they cannot reuse plastic forever. It will eventually end up in landfills. While this argument is comprehensible, it is not expressed well. For example, the student states that "reuse is important, but people do not reuse it." This statement should read: "Reusing is important, but people do not always reuse their products." Despite the grammatical errors, the idea is still unique from the other two discussion posts, and the student raises a point that was not considered in either of them: a product can only be reused for so long.

However, this cannot counteract the fact that almost every sentence contains a grammatical error. Specifically, the following sentence is unclear: "When you reuse things, you spend less money and there is less." Based on context, the general idea can be understood, but this phrasing is enough to make this response mid-level.

In order to be a high-level response, the writing would need to be much clearer, containing far fewer mistakes and none that make comprehension difficult. The vocabulary would also have to be more comprehensive. This writer tends to fall back on the word "important" to clarify every point, which is ineffective in formal writing.

Transcripts of Recordings for Test #1

Listening Passage 1: Conversation Transcript

Narrator: Listen to the following conversation between two students and then answer the following questions.

Male student: Hi Claudia, how's your philosophy class?

Female student: Oh, hey Miguel, it's pretty good. I love the material we are learning but I'm frustrated with a big assignment that's due next week.

Male student: Oh no. Why's that?

Female student: Well, it's a group project and we have to write a 10-page paper and prepare a 20-minute presentation about different notable philosophers, but my group doesn't seem to be taking the assignment seriously.

Male student: That sounds stressful. Does it count for a large percentage of your course grade?

Female student: Yes, that's the thing. This is our midterm project so it is worth 40% of our total grade. It's due on Monday and two of the people have yet to start their sections and the other student's piece was terrible.

Male student: Oh ... what was wrong with it?

Female student: It really didn't satisfy any of the assignment requirements. His job was to cover Aristotle. Our professor gave us specific criteria to address for each philosopher, like where and when they were born, their primary ideas and interests, and who they influenced and who influenced them. Brian, the guy in my group, just focused on Ancient Greece in general and barely mentioned Aristotle, let alone his philosophical contributions!

Male students: That's awful. You know, that's the reason why I find group projects to be stressful. You never know who is going to be in your group and how motivated they are. Sometimes you end up having to do the nearly the whole project yourself or settle for a poor grade. Last year in my engineering class we had to design a suspension bridge using renewable resources in small groups. I had to carry the weight of the whole group since no one held up their end. It was so much work to do by myself.

Female student: Yeah ... not fair. I might have to do that for this project. Before this, I always loved group projects, but now my opinion has shifted.

Male student: Well Claudia, I wish you luck with the project. I don't envy the situation you're in.

Female student: Thanks for commiserating with me, Miguel. Have a nice afternoon.

Listening Passage 2: Lecture Transcript

Narrator: Listen to the following part of a lecture on Sensory Processing Disorder from an education class.

Male professor: Ok everyone. Let's settle down and get started. Today, we are continuing our discussion of different developmental and neurological disorders that your future students may have. We are going to turn our attention to Sensory Processing Disorder, or SPD, which is increasingly entering into the dialogue of educators, as awareness and diagnosis increase. In addition to affecting the five senses (touch, smell, taste, vision, and hearing), SPD can manifest in issues with proprioception, vestibular function, and interoception, which is one's awareness of internal stimuli like hunger. I want to stress that SPD has a variety of presentations and it's likely that any two students in your classrooms with SPD may seem almost more different from one another than the same!

Individuals with SPD can be sensory-defensive or sensory-seeking, although these two are not always um ... mutually exclusive. For example, someone may be sensory defensive when it comes to auditory stimuli, in which case, he or she has a very low tolerance for noises and becomes easily overwhelmed with sounds. That same person may be a sensory seeker with movement, and constantly desire movement and pressure. It is much more common that a person is either a seeker or defensive though. In general, sensory seekers have a very high threshold for the sensory stimuli; they need a lot of it for their brain to process the signal and feel satisfied. Those who are sensory defensive have very low thresholds, so they cannot tolerate much input before becoming overwhelmed or even physically ill.

In addition to issues with thresholds for sensory stimuli, there are often issues integrating the sensory information. Actually, the disorder used to be called sensory integration disorder, so some of you may have heard of that terminology instead. Anyway, integration issues can manifest in a variety of ways because there are several senses and the reliance on them overlaps in most situations. For example, it's very rare that you only see something but there is no auditory input, or that you'd taste something without also having some degree of smell input. With integration issues, sometimes it is these combinations that create issues with interpreting the signal. More often, there is an issue processing a given type of input. For example, someone with SPD may hear an annoying sound but completely lack the ability to point to the direction in which it is coming.

The impact of SPD on an individual can be far-reaching because of the number of senses and the way in which they interact in an integrated way normally, to help us make sense of our environment and our body within the environment. Those with sensory-defensiveness tend to get easily overwhelmed and physically uncomfortable and normal, everyday environments like classrooms, shopping centers, and even the home, because everything is essentially "too much" – too loud, too bright, too chaotic, etc.

Young children who are unable to fully express their feelings are often seen as picky, immature, or out-of-control. In the toddler population, kids with SPD are often tantruming, they may experience late potty training, they can be hard to calm and have difficulty sleeping, and sensory seekers are often found crashing into things, jumping, eating ice, yelling, etc. In the classroom, students with SPD often have issues with handwriting, copying from the board, tolerating noisy lunchrooms, making smooth transitions, and having a good awareness of their body's position in space.

Occupational therapy, which you may have heard referred to as OT, is the most frequently cited specialized service to help students with SPD cope with symptoms and be more comfortable. The therapist can work with the student and also advise the parents and teachers of modifications and techniques to facilitate the student's comfort. The specific OT services that a student may receive vary according to their needs and presentation of the disorder as well as any concomitant challenges.

Actually, that's another important point to emphasize. Sensory Processing Disorder is often accompanied by other learning disorders or behavioral and developmental issues, such as autism,

ADHD, and anxiety disorders. If students have concurrent disorders, or what we refer to as comorbidities, these should be considered in conjunction when determining classroom accommodations and overall treatment. Your textbook does a good job covering suggested classroom accommodations for all sorts of SPD-related challenges, so let's review particular OT strategies and classroom modifications next class after your reading assignment.

Listening Passage 3: Lecture Transcript

Narrator: Listen to part of a lecture from a world religions class and then answer the questions.

Female professor: So, recall that we've been looking at how Buddhism in China has evolved in many different directions. Adapting the religion from its Indian origins into a uh ... Chinese context had inherent difficulties, due to the differences in culture, language, and epistemologies. This left Buddhism in an especially malleable state in China, which um ... provides some explanation as to how so many different forms of Buddhism came to exist. Each branch of Buddhism takes a different approach in the recruitment and education of followers. When followers of the same religion begin to disagree on fundamental issues, the religion inevitably splits to form two new interpretations of the original. Today, we are going to talk about the first of these splits, which resulted in the formation of the Mahayana and Theravada branches of Buddhism.

Theravada Buddhism is based on the "Four Noble Truths": all known existence is suffering, suffering is caused by desire, one must eliminate desire to eliminate suffering, and one must follow the eightfold path in order to eliminate desire. This eightfold path consisted of maintaining the Right View, Right Intention, Right Speech, Right Action, Right Livelihood, Right Effort, Right Mindfulness, and uh ... Right Concentration. Theravada Buddhism focused a great deal on the last section of the eightfold path, which was meditation, so a great deal of one's time was to be dedicated to deep mediation. This made Theravada Buddhism an esoteric religion because the people of the lower and middle classes were unable to devote so much time to meditation. Essentially, only the um ... highest classes were able to dedicate their lives to this, because they were the only classes with sufficient leisure time.

Mahayana Buddhists believed that the Theravada form was inaccessible to the great majority of people, due to the extreme emphasis on meditation. The Mahayana Buddhists disagreed so much with the Theravada Buddhists that they even referred to Theravada as Hinayana, or "The Lesser Vehicle."

Actually, this is an important distinction and warrants a pause in our discussion just to reiterate. Theravada and Mahayana Buddhism differ to a great extent in the basic ideology of attracting new followers. Theravada essentially makes little effort to include those who are unable to adhere to the requirements of their religion. The Mahayana Buddhists designed their religion to appeal to a great number of people, you know, basically to be more convenient and understandable to the illiterate masses.

I know we've only just started to scratch the surface here and there is a lot of layers we'll get to uncover about these sects in the coming days, but in an effort to not overwhelm you, let's end here a bit early and pick up next class.

Listening Passage 4: Lecture and Discussion Transcript

Narrator: Listen to the following portion of a lecture and discussion from a statistics class.

Male Professor: So, recall that we've been looking at the hierarchy of the four scales of measurement we use in research, which will be important for you to consider as you design your own experiments and evaluate research. As a quick review, we have nominal, ordinal, interval, and ratio. Nominal scales are the lowest level of measurement. We also refer to them as classificatory scales, wherein objects or people are assigned to categories according to some criterion. Ordinal scale measurements require categories to be rank ordered on the basis of an operationally-defined characteristic or property. For example, customer satisfaction ranked 1 to 5. Interval scales possess the rank order characteristics of an ordinal scale but there are known equal distances between consecutive units of measurement. This allows relative differences in equivalences within a scale to be determined. Ratio scales achieve the greatest measurement specificity. A ratio scale is an interval scale with an absolute zero point that has empirical, rather than an arbitrary, meaning.

Today I want us to consider the relevance and importance of assessing accuracy and precision within each of these scales. Before we do this though, who is willing to remind us about what accuracy and reliability mean? Yes, Janet.

Female student: Well, uh ... accuracy refers to the closeness of a measured value to a standard or known value. For example, hmmm ... if you obtain a weight measurement of 3.8 kilograms for a given substance, but the actual weight is 10 kilograms , then your measurement is not accurate. Precision, on the other hand, refers to like the closeness of two or more measurements of the same item to each other. Using the same example, if you weigh a given object five times, and get 3.6 kilograms each time, then your measurement is very precise.

Male professor: Very well said, Janet and those examples were perfect. And remember, precision is independent of accuracy. You can be very precise but inaccurate and you can be accurate but imprecise. So now, let's try to layer this thinking onto our different measurement scales and evaluate them through the lens of their potential accuracy and precision. I'll start with nominal scales and then see if anyone wants to take a stab at any of the others. Ok? Because nominal scales are more like categories, it is hard to have much precision. For example, if the categories are various colors, our values could be blue, red, and green. But, the categories will have many shades of each color that all have a common general color but many variations of the hue. Sky blue and navy look very different, right? Accuracy would also be challenging. Continuing with our color example, the delineations between the categories are not very specific. There can be shades of blue that also appear green, such as teal, so which category would they go in? One investigator could select green while another chooses blue.

So, let's consider ordinal scales. Remember, they are represented by rank orders divided by intervals that are not always consistent or known. Two subjects assigned in the same rank may in fact be of completely different values. The ordinal scale is not sensitive enough to determine the differences between ranks and is only able to indicate a relative position of certain distribution rather than its true value or quantity. Manual muscle test is an ordinal scale test. Assigning a grade to an individual may be very accurate and precise based on the scale. However, this scale is pretty much useless when comparing two or more individuals since the difference between two scores is hard to be defined. Who is willing to stick their neck out and try interval scales?

Male student: Interval scales are essentially an intermediary between the lack of specificity of nominal and ordinal but a little less defined than ratio with no absolute zero, so I think we cannot be quite as precise as ratio but more than the lower levels of measurement. My hunch is that the artificial zero point that these scales possess decrease its accuracy because the zero points are just arbitrarily chosen.

Male professor: You hit the nail on the head, Donovan! Who wants to try ratio?

Female student: Well, I think because there are essentially an infinite number of values along the continuum in the ratio scale, it is easier to be more precise because the difference from one value to the next is very, very small. I'm not sure about accuracy.

Male professor: Great start. You've hit on an important concept. In general, scales of higher forms of measurement are more precise. Accuracy is also more important in scales like interval and ratio that are higher levels of measurement and may have more specificity to their assigned values. In a sense, the target on the bullseye is smaller, so it seems logical that it would be easier to miss it and be inaccurate more frequently than in large sweeping general categories like nominal and ordinal scales. For instance, we know gender is nominal. It's generally easy to identify someone as male or female so you are less likely to make a mistake. Salary is a ratio measurement and since there are essentially an infinite number of salaries, it would be easier to misreport it and have an accuracy error. Perhaps you inadvertently flip the numbers around, or mishear a fifty as sixty.

Listening Passage 5: Conversation Transcript

Narrator: Listen to the following conversation between a student and his professor and then answer the questions.

Female professor: Hey Connor, thanks for staying after class. I won't keep you long, but I wanted to talk about your grades and progress in my course.

Male student: Yeah, I've been meaning to come to your office hours for some help. I guess I'm struggling to understand the chemistry material.

Female professor: Well, I'm glad you are trying to be proactive about your studies and yes, you should always feel free to come to my office hours. If those times don't work for you, I am also happy to meet with you at an alternative time.

Male student: Thanks, but they are fine. I can come on Tuesdays and Thursdays after my trigonometry class. Availability wasn't the limiting factor; I think it was my pride.

Female professor: I appreciate your honesty and don't worry, a lot of students are nervous or shy to ask for help. But the good news is, you are here now we can start addressing your challenges. So, on the last exam, you got a 62. You got most of the questions about acids and bases correct, but it looks like you didn't get any of the chemical structure and bonding questions.

Male student: Yeah, balancing chemical equations went completely over my head and I don't understand the differences between ionic, covalent, and hydrogen bonds.

Female professor: Have you tried looking at this material in the course textbook?

Male student: I tried, but I found the writing to be very dense and the examples were confusing.

Female professor: OK. Don't worry. We have a lot of alternative resources that can help you. I'd like you to start coming to my office hours twice a week after your trigonometry class. Additionally, I think he would benefit from going to the Student Resource Center.

Male student: Hmm ... what's that?

Female professor: It's a room in the library on the second floor with all of the reference materials. The University has a bunch of paid tutors who work with students in a variety of subjects. It's free for all undergraduate students because it is included in your tuition bill, and graduate students just pay a nominal fee.

Male student: Wow, that sounds great! I had no idea that we had a resource like that on campus. Do they have chemistry tutors?

Female professor: Yes. There are several great tutors to cover all of the sciences, including chemistry. I will fill out a referral form for you. All you need to do is call or stop by the Student Resource Center and set up an appointment. They will ask you for the referral form and your student ID.

Male student: Perfect. Thanks, Professor Winter. I'll get right on this.

Female professor: That's great, Connor. There is still plenty of time left in the semester to turn your grade around.

Speaking Passage 1: Conversation Transcript

Narrator: Listen to the following conversation between two students regarding school parking policies.

Male student: Hey Janice, did you read about the new parking policy starting in the fall?

Female student: No, I don't drive so I must have skimmed over it. What's happening, Adam?

Male student: Well, the University's Public Safety and Parking Services department decided that starting next year, freshman and sophomore students cannot buy a campus parking permit. Only juniors and seniors will be able to have their cars here. I'm so mad! I'm only going to be a sophomore, so I won't get to keep my car on campus anymore.

Female student: Oh wow! Well, you know, it's actually probably a good idea because there are fewer parking spaces now that they put in the baseball field and it's kind of an unfair advantage for students who don't have financial limitations. I heard they are like $500 a year!

Male student: Yeah, I think they are like $550, but if you can afford it, you should be able to buy one. Plus, it's not like I just use my car myself. I take my roommate and buddies from my dorm out to the movies or to play billiards. They always want rides!

Female student: That sounds fun but you know, the Campus Center has movies every night except Monday and there is a big game room on the second floor with pool tables, air hockey, and foosball. It's really fun. Plus, all this stuff is free.

Male student: I didn't know there was a game room but I bet the movies they show are lame. I like watching movies in the theater. It's a really nice break from being stuck on campus all the time.

Female student: I hear you, but the movie selections they play are actually really good and they're always relatively new releases. Oh, and also, there is the free campus shuttle bus that runs to the shopping mall, grocery store, movie theater, and uh, the downtown area. You could always hop on that to go to the movies.

Male student: Yeah, I guess. I've actually never taken that. I just like driving because you can go whenever you want and aren't slave to the bus schedule.

Female student: Well come try it with me and my friends on Friday! We are going to check out a new cafe downtown. They have karaoke!

Male student: Ok. Maybe. Thanks Janice.

Speaking Passage 2: Lecture Transcript

Professor: So, theory of mind is somewhat similar to empathy, though it expands on this concept by taking it a step further. An effective theory of mind arms the person with the ability to understand and even predict another person's reactions, actions, and feelings. This enables someone to have more meaningful, and arguably, more compassionate and empathetic social interactions by allowing people engaging with one another to attribute thoughts, moods, and intentions to others, to predict or explain their actions and desires. As your text pointed out, these skills, along with perspective-taking and empathy, begin to develop in infancy and are strengthened with healthy and stable social engagement and language exposure. However, when a person has cognitive or developmental disorders, he or she may struggle with theory of mind. Although it's not a hard-and-fast rule, individuals with autism spectrum disorder often demonstrate incomplete or ineffective theories of mind and difficulty with empathy. In graduate school, I did my dissertation on autism and empathy. One young woman I worked with lacked a completely developed theory of mind. She often misinterpreted the feelings and intentions of her peers. She frequently thought that other people hated her when they did not indicate that, and she struggled to understand that other people's opinions and experiences could differ from her own. For example, while she loved talking about computer games, she would become agitated and angry when other people did not demonstrate this passion or didn't have the extensive knowledge base regarding computer games that she had.

Speaking Passage 3: Lecture Transcript

Professor: What is a species? Now, this is a hard question because there are many schools of thought on this subject, but let's use the biological species concept. This concept defines a species as a group of individuals, be it animals, plants, what have you, living in one or more populations. According to this definition of species, the members of a species should be able to interbreed and produce healthy offspring that can, in turn, reproduce.

However, we all know that species can adapt to the environment through the process of natural selection. This often results in speciation events, in which an ancestral group splits into two or more distinct groups, or species. When speciation occurs, the newly formed groups are unable to reproduce due to their differences in behavior, chromosomes, and habit, among other reasons as well.

It's important to note that there are two kinds of speciation events: allopatric and sympatric speciation. As root words, *allo* means *other*, and *patric* means *land* or *homeland*. Taking the etymology into consideration, we can infer that this kind of speciation occurs when a group of organisms becomes physically separated from others in the group. This kind of physical barrier can be anything from a rockslide to lava to a river. Often when groups become physically separated, they undergo what's called genetic divergence, meaning that they become different genetically. As discussed, this happens due to natural selection favoring certain traits in the environment. Keep in mind that the groups are typically only considered new species when they no longer are able to reproduce even if they reunite.

Sympatric speciation, on the other hand, actually occurs on the *sym*, or same, land. That sounds strange. How is that even possible? Well, we don't really see this type of speciation in animals, but it is common in plants. Plants sometimes undergo a process in which they end up with more than two sets of chromosomes. This is incredibly unlikely, almost impossible, in animals, but plants seem to be resistant to these types of changes. During certain reproduction events, the parent chromosomes simply fail to separate correctly, leading to a plant with too much genetic information to appropriately mate with others of its parent species. It is considered a new species.

Writing Passage 1: Lecture Transcript

Male professor: The effects of social networking come with far too many risks. Many consumers are targeted with phishing schemes that steal people's money or even their identity. These risks do not only extend to adults, but also to children, who are targeted for bullying and manipulation. Children can easily pick up deficits from becoming too reliant on social media for communication. People these days already have a lack of social skills from looking at screens each day. This has already made a clear impact on family systems in America.

A new study by sociologists at Duke University and the University of Arizona adds more grist to this mill, noting that Americans in 2004 had smaller networks of people with whom they talk about matters important to them than they did in 1985. In 1985, the average American had three close confidants. In 2004, we averaged only two. The number of Americans who had no one with whom to talk about important matters almost doubled in 2004, to over 25%. Increasingly, most confidants are family: in 2004, 80% of people talked only to family about important matters, and about 9% depended totally on their spouse.

This decrease in confidants is in part a result of the same trend that's leaving fewer people knowing their neighbors or participating in social clubs or public affairs than in the past. We know a lot of people, but we don't know them very well.

Left to our own devices and cultural trends then, we seem to be moving in an unpleasant direction. Communities are formed ad hoc, around specific shared individual interests. This wouldn't be bad, of course, except that those communities seem to exist only within the constraints of those shared interests, and don't develop into close and meaningful relationships. The transient and specific nature of many of our relationships today can keep us socially busy without building the lasting relationships and communities that we want.

TOEFL Practice Test #2

Reading

Additional Instructions for the Test

When you take the real test, you will be given a university-level text. After fully reading the text, you will be able to access the questions. During this time, you will be able to refer back to the passage while answering the questions. You will have two reading passages during your test and 36 minutes to complete both passages. Take your time and remember that all of the answers can be found in the passage.

Questions 1–10 are based on the following passage.

Passage 1

(1) Land plants have biological defense systems that increase their resistance to and defend against bacteria, fungi, and other organisms or pathogens that pose a threat to their well-being. One of these defense systems is the salicylic acid pathway. For many years, it was thought that pathogenesis-related (PR) gene expression and enhanced resistance to certain pathogens could only be induced by the application of salicylic acid, but it was then discovered in the early 1990s that salicylic acid is an endogenous (made in the plant) compound that operates locally and systemically in plants as a signal transduction pathway (how cells communicate) related to disease resistance responses. This pathway is now referred to as systemic acquired resistance (SAR) and is known to be dependent on salicylic acid. The SAR pathway is initiated in response to the presence of a pathogen; when pathogenic proteins interact with specific recognition mechanisms, the SAR pathway is initiated in order to isolate the pathogen from the rest of the plant as a mechanism of providing even distant, uninfected plant parts with resistance to a broad range of pathogens. Defense-related genes that produce lignin, suberin, phenylpropanoids, and phytoalexins are then activated, leading to cell wall rigidification, synthesis of phytoalexins, and the accumulation of PR proteins like hydrolytic enzymes. The activation of these genes also contributes to greater viral, bacterial, and fungal resistance in other, unaffected parts of the plant. After the SAR pathway has been initiated, PR genes in parts of the uninfected tissue of the plant become expressed; however, not all PR genes are expressed in response to the salicylic SAR pathway—in fact, some PR genes rely on completely different catalysts for their expression.

(2) There are some plants, such as transgenic *NahG* plants, that encode an enzyme that breaks down salicylic acid. Plants with these limitations must rely on another defense pathway, specifically that of jasmonic acid and ethylene. When a plant is invaded by a pathogen, both of these signaling molecules are produced locally and systemically, a system in which jasmonic acid is carried to systemic tissues. Ethylene and jasmonic acid activate the expression of pathogenesis-related genes that encode defensins and thionins (PR proteins), which in turn assist in antimicrobial activity and enhance systemic resistance much like the salicylic pathway does. This pathway, since it is independent of the salicylic acid pathway, is called induced systemic resistance (ISR). Based on work with gene-knockout mutants in *Arabidopsis* (a plant), SAR and ISR are proposed to <u>confer</u> resistance to pathogens according to their methods of infection, in that SAR primarily functions against biotrophic pathogens and ISR against necrotrophic pathogens. Due to the two pathways' functions, many plants have and use both the salicylic and jasmonic/ethylene pathways in conjunction.

(3) Studies have shown that when plants initiate defensive pathways, their neighbors often feel the effects either by commencing their own defensive pathways or by being primed, meaning that they are more readily able to initiate defense pathways despite not having been in contact with the other plant. Many researchers have based their experiments on the possibility of airborne communication, pinpointing volatile organic compounds (VOCs) known as methyl jasmonate (MeJA), a derivative of jasmonic acid; ethylene; and methyl salicylate (MeSA), a derivative of salicylic acid, that have the potential to elicit defense responses in other plants when received through the air. Due to the tendency of VOCs to dissipate in the air, the distance between donor and receiver plants has to be quite minimal for the airborne signals to have an effect.

(4) This, however, is not the case when defense signals are transferred via mycorrhizal fungi. Around 90 percent of land plants have underground mycorrhizal associations, which are symbiotic relationships between plant roots and fungi. These associations are formed by two fungal symbionts: arbuscular mycorrhizal fungi (AMF) or ectomycorrhizal (ECM) fungi. These relationships typically benefit the host plants by increasing nutrient and water uptake because the thin nature of the fungi allows them to be exposed to more soil per volume. In addition, many of these fungi can fix nitrogen and phosphorus from the soil or atmosphere into a usable form for their plant hosts, resulting in a mutualistic relationship. Mycorrhizae can be <u>selective</u> when it comes to their hosts; many only pair with specific plants, but others, typically AMF, are less selective. Less selective mycorrhizae are more likely to form common mycorrhizal networks (CMNs), which form when the fungal mycelia of two or more plants, either the same or different species, link together via hyphal fusions. Carbon, nitrogen, phosphorus, and water are products transferred between plants through mycorrhizal associations, a service that could be lifesaving when faced with drought and resource scarcity. Along with nutrient transfer, CMNs also provide a degree of protection against pathogens and have been shown to transfer defense signals between plants of the same and different species. Due to the many ecosystem services they provide, mycorrhizal networks are essential for a productive and biodiverse ecosystem.

1. The activation of defense-related genes contributes to all of the following EXCEPT:

a. Stronger resistance against bacterial infection
b. The production of suberin
c. Stronger resistance against wind damage
d. Reinforcing of the cell wall

2. Which of the following expresses how mycorrhizae benefit plants?

a. Fungi transfer defense signals to neighboring plants.
b. Fungi help plants choose the right host for the common mycorrhizal networks.
c. Fungi benefit from plants because fungi receive sugars made from photosynthesis.
d. Fungi are capable of protecting themselves from bacteria.

3. Why did the author choose to include the following sentence in paragraph 1?

"Defense-related genes that produce lignin, suberin, phenylpropanoids, and phytoalexins are then activated, leading to cell wall rigidification, synthesis of phytoalexins, and the accumulation of PR proteins like hydrolytic enzymes."

a. To compare salicylic acid and jasmonic acid in defense responses
b. To disprove the claim that the SAR pathway uses proteins in its defense response
c. To give examples of the mechanisms the SAR pathway deploys in fighting pathogens
d. To suggest that the salicylic acid pathway is not effective at reducing biological threats

4. Why did the author choose to include the following sentence in paragraph 4?

"Around 90 percent of land plants have underground mycorrhizal associations, which are symbiotic relationships between plant roots and fungi."

a. To suggest the drawbacks of fungal symbiosis with plants
b. To give an example of the types of plants that have mycorrhizal connections
c. To provide a foundational understanding of defense signals
d. To illustrate the importance of mycorrhizal fungi

5. The word *confer* in paragraph 2 is closest in meaning to:

a. Possess
b. Grant
c. Deny
d. Converse

6. The word *selective* in paragraph 4 is closest in meaning to:

a. General
b. Cautious
c. Indiscriminate
d. Particular

7. Which of the sentences below best expresses the most important information in the following sentence from paragraph 1?

"The SAR pathway is initiated in response to the presence of a pathogen; when pathogenic proteins interact with specific recognition mechanisms, the SAR pathway is initiated in order to isolate the pathogen from the rest of the plant as a mechanism of providing even distant, uninfected plant parts with resistance to a broad range of pathogens."

a. The SAR pathway sections off the plant from others so that the infection won't reach other plants in the population.
b. The purpose of the SAR pathway is to isolate the infection so that the entire plant is less likely to become diseased.
c. Certain pathogens cause the SAR pathway to begin in plants, which leads the plants to perish quickly.
d. Plants may be able to start the SAR pathway in response to some pathogens, but others remain undetected in the plant systems.

8. Which of the sentences below best expresses the most important information in the following sentence from paragraph 3?

"Many researchers have based their experiments on the possibility of airborne communication, pinpointing volatile organic compounds (VOCs) known as methyl jasmonate (MeJA), a derivative of jasmonic acid; ethylene; and methyl salicylate (MeSA), a derivative of salicylic acid, that have the potential to elicit defense responses in other plants when received through the air."

a. Scientists believe that certain airborne compounds in plants have the ability to evoke defense responses in their neighbors.
b. The role of methyl jasmonate, ethylene, and methyl salicylate in inducing defense responses in pathogens is being studied.
c. Plants have the ability to produce defense responses in volatile organic compounds.
d. Experts have found some airborne toxins that interact negatively with plants.

9. There is a missing sentence in paragraph 2, which is reproduced below. Where would this sentence fit best?

"These plants, therefore, lack the ability to accumulate salicylic acid and, as a result, do not develop an SAR response."

[1] There are some plants, such as transgenic *NahG* plants, that encode an enzyme that breaks down salicylic acid. [2] Plants with these limitations must rely on another defense pathway, specifically that of jasmonic acid and ethylene. [3] When a plant is invaded by a pathogen, both of these signaling molecules are produced locally and systemically, a system in which jasmonic acid is carried to systemic tissues. [4] Ethylene and jasmonic acid activate the expression of pathogenesis-related genes that encode defensins and thionins (PR proteins), which in turn assist in antimicrobial activity and enhance systemic resistance much like the salicylic pathway does.

a. [1]
b. [2]
c. [3]
d. [4]

10. Choose the THREE sentences below that provide an accurate single-sentence summary of a main idea of the passage.

a. Mycorrhizae perform important roles for plants by transferring chemical signals and nutrients.
b. Plants have biological mechanisms that help them fight off pathogens.
c. Volatile organic compounds fade into the air before they reach other plants.
d. Plants that have initiated their own defensive pathways can trigger these pathways in their neighbors.
e. Plants can use either the SAR pathway or the ISR pathway to respond to biotic threats, but not both.
f. Fungi only connect with specific plants, which can negatively affect the environment.

Questions 11–20 are based on the following passage.

PASSAGE 2

(1) Phrenology was a pseudoscientific study developed in the late 18th and early 19th century by the German physician Franz Joseph Gall. The main belief of this discipline was that a person's psychological characteristics—such as secretiveness, combativeness, and cautiousness—could be determined by his or her cranial structure, or the shape of the skull. Following this ideology, the brain was divided into many regions that defined a personality, and the size of a cranial area was directly related to the development of a specific quality; this is to say that the larger the area, the more developed the feature. To examine the areas, phrenologists ran their fingers or palms over an individual's head to distinguish elevations and depressions in the skull; however, a caliper or tape measure could also be used. Gall identified 27 cranial areas or "organs" that he referred to as the brain regions responsible for personality traits.

(2) To <u>corroborate</u> his beliefs, Gall collected animal and human skulls and calculated the sizes of their cranial protuberances. Most of the skulls he collected were of people known to have specific characteristics in life, which may have influenced Gall's objectivity. However, phrenology became very popular in Europe and the United States. A phrenological society was founded in Edinburgh, but by the mid-19th century, the practice had been discredited in the scientific

community. Although most of Gall's theories were baseless, and phrenology is considered a pseudoscience given the lack of supporting scientific evidence, the basis of Gall's theories was not entirely wrong. There are areas of specialization in the brain, but the brain does not grow outward or affect the skull. Furthermore, there are no phrenological "organs," but by chance, Gall's language "organ" was located near the part of the brain that is now known as the part that controls language.

(3) In 1861, the French neurologist and anthropologist Pierre Paul Broca wrote about a patient who was unable to express himself with language. An autopsy showed that a wound had impaired part of his left hemisphere's frontal lobe, which, upon further observation, led Broca to theorize that the left frontal lobe is the "seat" of human language. Carl Wernicke, another neurologist, described patients with damaged left hemispheres whose speech was fluent but had no informational value, described as "fluent nonsense." Wernicke came to a similar conclusion as Broca: linguistic mental function is localized in the cerebral cortex and involves only the left hemisphere. This leads to a functional asymmetry between the two hemispheres, which is linked to the dominant hand. Thus, the left hemisphere controls the right half of the body, making the left hemisphere dominant for right-handed people.

(4) To study this phenomenon, patients with a brain disease or traumatic injury were presented with various tasks like completing mathematical equations or copying drawings. The tasks that a patient could not complete well were associated with the part of his or her brain that was damaged. This study methodology took a long time to complete because the researchers had to wait until the patient died of natural causes to examine his or her brain in autopsy. Now that scientists have developed neuroimaging and other technologies, it is easier to study brain damage in a living patient. These studies have confirmed some of Broca's and Wernicke's theories. Neurologists today uphold the idea that the brain has specialized functions in different areas, including language; however, the two hemispheres work together more than separately.

(5) Scientists have discovered that the right and left brain hemispheres are connected by a large band of myelinated nerve fibers called the corpus callosum. Partial functional asymmetry is based on the idea that the left brain controls cognitive and behavioral functions, while the right brain controls creative functions. Many believe, although data is insufficient, that the structural asymmetry between the two hemispheres is the basis of different linguistic skills and manual mastery, which is known as hemispheric specialization.

(6) The left hemisphere, for example, controls language-related functions such as the use of semantics and grammar, along with analytical reasoning, problem-solving, and interpretive ability. It also controls fine motor movements in the hands, fingers, arms, and the muscles that help articulate speech. Broca and Wernicke discovered damage to the left hemisphere in patients that had had difficulty with both word recognition and communication with others. On the other hand, the right hemisphere has greater effects on the processing of socio-emotional information, as it is more connected to the limbic system and predominantly controls the sympathetic nervous system. It manages all functions related to the perception and expression of emotions through gestures and words along with playing an important role in visuospatial tasks such as orientation in space and processing sensations. Damage to the right hemisphere may prevent a patient from recognizing familiar faces and objects.

11. According to the passage, which of Gall's theories below was NOT false?

a. The brain grows outward.
b. The brain affects the development of the skull.
c. Scientists can predict behavior based on cranial structure.
d. There are areas of specialization in the brain.

12. To which conclusion did Carl Wernicke's and Pierre Paul Broca's research lead?

a. The left hemisphere controls language function.
b. People with brain damage in either the left or right hemisphere will lose language function.
c. The best way to analyze brain damage is to perform autopsies on dead patients.
d. The right and left hemispheres control different aspects of language.

13. Why did the author choose to include the following sentence in paragraph 4?

"This study methodology took a long time to complete because the researchers had to wait until the patient died of natural causes to examine his or her brain in autopsy."

a. To contrast Wernicke's and Broca's research methods
b. To illustrate an obstacle scientists had to face in the past
c. To disprove the assertion that technological invention is necessary for science
d. To suggest that scientists are still struggling to understand brain function

14. Why did the author choose to include the following sentence in paragraph 6?

"Broca and Wernicke discovered damage to the left hemisphere in patients that had had difficulty with both word recognition and communication with others."

a. To prove that the left hemisphere has little effect on language function
b. To acknowledge the difference between Broca's and Wernicke's discoveries
c. To provide an example of left hemisphere functionality
d. To suggest that the left hemisphere is only responsible for language

15. The word *corroborate* in paragraph 2 is closest in meaning to:

a. Publicize
b. Contradict
c. Understand
d. Support

16. The word *impaired* in paragraph 3 is closest in meaning to:

a. Dissected
b. Damaged
c. Dulled
d. Encouraged

17. Which of the sentences below best expresses the most important information in the following sentence from paragraph 1?

"Following this ideology, the brain was divided into many regions that defined a personality, and the size of a cranial area was directly related to the development of a specific quality; this is to say that the larger the area, the more developed the feature."

a. Phrenology states that if someone has a large bump on his or her skull, he or she will have a more interesting personality.
b. During autopsies, the brain would be divided into many pieces so that the scientists could understand how the deceased individual's personality was formed.
c. Different sections of the brain control personality traits that can be measured based on the size of the skull's bumps.
d. The brain itself is not whole but several separate organs that each control several personality traits.

18. Which of the sentences below best expresses the most important information in the following sentence from paragraph 5?

"Many believe, although data is insufficient, that the structural asymmetry between the two hemispheres is the basis of different linguistic skills and manual mastery, which is known as hemispheric specialization."

a. The two parts of the brain are responsible for different tasks and developmental skills, but this theory has not been proven.
b. Although scientists have little proof, many believe that the hemispheres of the brain perform the same functions and are, therefore, analogous.
c. In many people, one half of the brain is larger, which means that it is the dominant side.
d. A lot of data suggests that certain parts of the brain are dedicated to different tasks, but scientists have not accepted this theory.

19. There is a missing sentence in paragraph 5, which is reproduced below. Where would this sentence fit best?

"The corpus callosum allows the two hemispheres to cooperate even though there are distinctions between their psychological functions."

[1] Scientists have discovered that the right and left brain hemispheres are connected by a large band of myelinated nerve fibers called the corpus callosum. [2] Partial functional asymmetry is based on the idea that the left brain controls cognitive and behavioral functions, while the right brain controls creative functions. [3] Many believe, although data is insufficient, that the structural asymmetry between the two hemispheres is the basis of different linguistic skills and manual mastery, which is known as hemispheric specialization. [4]

a. [1]
b. [2]
c. [3]
d. [4]

20. Choose the THREE sentences below that provide an accurate single-sentence summary of a main idea of the passage.

a. Phrenology was the study of psychological characteristics on the basis of cranial shape.
b. The left hemisphere controls emotion, whereas the right hemisphere controls language.
c. Phrenology is supported by scientific research and has been widely accepted.
d. Scientists discovered that the capacity for language is controlled by specific parts of the brain.
e. Recent developments in science have made it easier to study the brain's function.
f. The left and right hemispheres have nearly the same functionality.

Listening

Additional Instructions for the Test

There are two types of listening samples in the listening portion of the TOEFL: short lectures and conversations. There are four to six short lectures and two to three conversations, each ranging from three to five minutes long. When you take the real test, you will first see a photo that should help orient you to the material, followed by an audio clip of either a conversation or a lecture. While the audio is playing, you should take notes. Try to identify main points if possible. After listening to the audio clip, you will be given five to six multiple choice questions. **You will not be given a transcript or be allowed to listen to the recording again.** A transcript of each conversation and lecture is included for your reference after the answer explanations.

Refer to the following for questions 1 - 6:

Listening passage 1: A lecture by a female professor

Practice Audio: Listening Passage 1: Lecture
Visit mometrix.com/academy and enter Code: 756602

1. What was the main topic of the lecture?

a. The importance of Shakespeare's plays
b. The complicated psychology of Lady Macbeth
c. The murder Macbeth committed
d. The reasons that people are manipulative

2. What does the professor mean when she says, "I can see I'm losing some of you,"

a. Her students do not agree with her argument.
b. Her students are dropping her course because it is too challenging.
c. Her students are about to graduate.
d. Her students are not focused on the lecture because they are worried about their exams.

3. Why might the professor say, "Do you guys see how the key to Lady Macbeth's strategy for gaining influence over her husband is to somewhat switch the gender roles within her marriage?" without pausing to call on her students for responses?

a. To help students stay focused and not get off topic answering questions
b. To encourage students to be critical thinkers as she strengthens her argument
c. To dominate the conversation and prevent interruptions
d. To remind the students that they have a lot to learn

4. What does the professor argue is a strength of Shakespeare's plays and a quality that made him a great playwright?

a. The fact that people have read his plays for centuries and his works are well-preserved
b. The fact that his works consider the complexities of human nature through character development
c. The fact that he persuades audience members to be deviant
d. The fact that his works teach readers about people and places from a vibrant period in history

5. The professor would likely describe Lady Macbeth as which of the following?

a. A very good and loyal wife
b. A very evil and manipulative wife
c. A character who is realistic in her psychological complexities
d. A predictable and mundane character

6. What is the professor's attitude about the character of Macbeth?

a. She thinks that he is easily swayed by his wife's dominant personality.
b. She thinks that he is a willing participant in the gender role reversal in his marriage.
c. She thinks that he is just as complex and realistic as Lady Macbeth.
d. She thinks that he manipulates his wife into murdering King Duncan.

Refer to the following for questions 7 - 11:

Listening passage 2: A conversation between a professor and a student

Practice Audio: Listening Passage 2: Conversation Visit mometrix.com/academy and enter Code: 108484

7. Why does the student go to see her professor?

a. To ask why there are no advanced Italian classes
b. To talk about doing an independent study
c. To discuss her previous translation work
d. To apply for extra credit

8. Why are there no advanced Italian classes this year?

a. The department has been cut.
b. Too few people signed up to take the class.
c. The professor who taught the course took another job.
d. Previous students complained about the teacher.

9. What kind of independent study would the student like to do?

a. A literature review of translated texts
b. A fieldwork study of translators at work
c. An analysis of the retranslation of popular texts
d. A translation of short stories

10. Which TWO answer choices reflect the expectations of an independent study?

a. The amount of work for each meeting depends on the difficulty of the text.
b. The student must contact the registrar to apply for five credits.
c. Weekly meetings will be focused on the student's progress.
d. The weekly meetings will last at least half an hour.

11. Review part of the conversation:

Female Student: I'm really looking for things that haven't been translated before and don't have a lot of literary critiques, so nothing too popular like Dante's *Divine Comedy*. I think retranslation is interesting, but I want to focus on more obscure texts that don't have much commentary yet.

Female Professor: I understand. The *Divine Comedy* has been worked to death at this point. You might want to focus on more regional tales.

Why does the professor say, "The *Divine Comedy* has been worked to death at this point"?

a. To suggest that the text has lost its meaning
b. To argue that the translators poorly interpreted the text
c. To show that retranslation is important
d. To emphasize that the text is overstudied

Refer to the following for questions 12 - 17:

Listening passage 3: A lecture by a female professor

Practice Audio: Listening Passage 3: Lecture
Visit mometrix.com/academy and enter Code: 108483

12. What is the lecture mainly about?

a. The transmission rate of genetic diseases
b. The pattern of autosomal dominant inheritance
c. The various kinds of diseases a person can inherit
d. The difference between autosomal and sex-linked traits

13. According to the professor, which TWO possibilities could result in a recessive trait's expression?

a. One parent is a carrier, and the other parent has the disorder.
b. One parent has a dominant disorder, and the other is not a carrier.
c. Both parents have the disorder.
d. One parent is a carrier, and the other is unaffected.

14. What does the professor illustrate with the example of brown eye color?

a. That recessive traits are expressed with only one allele
b. That two copies of the brown eye allele are necessary for its inheritance
c. That brown eyes are more common than blue eyes
d. That dominant traits override recessive traits

15. Why does the professor mention Huntington's disease?

a. To correct one of her student's assumptions about dominant disorders
b. To answer a question posed by a student
c. To give a concrete example of an autosomal dominant disorder
d. To contrast this disease with a recessive disorder mentioned previously

16. According to the professor, what is one big issue with Huntington's disease?

a. Those with the disease do not present symptoms.
b. It is a recessive disorder, which means it is more likely to be expressed.
c. People often don't know they are affected until later in life.
d. People with the disease rarely live past 50 years old.

17. Why does the professor say the following at the end of this part of the lecture?

"But what about recessive disorders? How do they present in the population, and how prevalent are they?"

a. She believes the students already know the answers to these questions.
b. She is trying to jog the students' memories of something she discussed earlier.
c. She is attempting to correct a mistake she has made in the lecture.
d. She wants to draw a comparison between dominant and recessive disorders.

Refer to the following for questions 18 - 23:

Listening passage 4: A lecture by a male professor

Practice Audio: Listening Passage 4: Lecture
Visit mometrix.com/academy and enter Code: 108482

18. What is the lecture mainly about?

a. The difference between classical and operant conditioning
b. Classical conditioning and its main principles
c. The various definitions of learning in scientific study
d. The way that behavior changes over time

19. According to the professor, how do behaviorists define learning?

a. A behavioral change in response to the environment
b. An innate ability to experience information
c. A conscious decision to change behavior
d. An automatic response to external stimuli

20. Which of the following is NOT true about classical conditioning?

a. There is a neutral stimulus associated with a different stimulus.
b. The learned reaction is automatic.
c. The learner will be aware of the behavioral change.
d. It was seen in the experiment of Pavlov's dogs.

21. Why does the professor discuss the example of a child and a barking dog?

a. To explain how Pavlov trained his dogs
b. To compare how children and animals learn
c. To demonstrate how fear can lead to avoidance in children
d. To illustrate the principle of learning as behavioral change

22. According to the professor, why did Pavlov's dogs salivate when the bell was rung?

a. The sound of the bell was associated with the food.
b. The dogs already had a response to the sound of the bell.
c. The sound of the bell made the dogs pay attention.
d. The dogs decided to salivate more when the bell rang.

23. In the following excerpt from the conversation, why does the professor say, "That's close"?

Female Student: Learning is like when you experience the environment.

Male Professor: That's close. Learning is defined as some kind of behavioral change that results from an interaction with the environment.

a. To encourage the student to continue her response
b. To illustrate that the student should correct herself
c. To assert that the student's response is an incomplete answer
d. To suggest that the student completely understands the answer

Refer to the following for questions 24 – 28:

Listening passage 5: A conversation between a professor and a student

Practice Audio: Listening Passage 5: Conversation
Visit mometrix.com/academy and enter Code: 108481

24. Why did the professor ask to talk to the student?

a. To discuss an issue with her classwork
b. To commend the student for her work
c. To give her instructions on how to complete the final project
d. To discuss an internship opportunity

25. What was noteworthy about the student's lab journal?

a. The student included unique specimen drawings.
b. The lab journal included incredibly detailed drawings and notes.
c. The student turned in her lab journal two weeks before it was due.
d. The lab journal had a beautiful cover illustration.

26. Why does the professor mention the security guard?

a. To offer a solution to a problem
b. To remind the student of the guard's responsibilities
c. To address an issue with the student's behavior
d. To explain why a problem was occurring

27. Which TWO of the following are tasks the student would perform in the internship?

a. Cataloging plant specimens
b. Conducting experiments
c. Preparing DNA samples
d. Performing DNA analysis

28. Why does the professor say, "Speaking of the end of the year, what are your plans for the summer"?

a. To see if the student has time to correct her final project
b. To motivate the student to continue studying over the summer
c. To suggest a travel vacation plan for the student
d. To transition to talk about an internship opportunity over the summer

Speaking

Additional Instructions for the Test

When you take the real test, you will have a variety of tasks to complete for the speaking section.

In question 1, you will answer a question that requires you to respond by speaking about your own experiences, ideas, and opinions. You will have 15 seconds to prepare and 45 seconds to respond.

In questions 2-4, you will listen to information and then speak your response to a question about that topic or read and listen to information about a topic and then speak your response to a question about that topic. You will have 20-30 seconds to prepare and 60 seconds to respond.

1. Some people think that standardized tests are the best way to gauge college readiness, but other people think that there are better ways to determine if a student is ready for college. What is your opinion? Explain your reasoning. Make sure to use specific details in your explanation.

Preparation Time: 15 seconds
Response Time: 45 seconds

2. Passage:

University officials have elected to reduce campus library hours for the foreseeable future. The campus library will now operate from 8 a.m. to 5 p.m. on weekdays, with no weekend hours. The administration has arrived at this decision due to a staffing shortage. Unfortunately, the university librarian has stepped down from his role for personal reasons. An interim librarian will take his place for the time being, but all acquisitions will be halted and many of the resources provided by the library will be discontinued. The administration is working hard to find a suitable replacement and will update the student body with every future development.

Speaking passage 1: A conversation between two students

Practice Audio: Speaking Passage 1: Conversation
Visit mometrix.com/academy and enter Code: 108480

Question: The male student expressed his opinion about the reduced library hours. State his opinion and explain the reasons he gives for holding that opinion.

Preparation Time: 30 seconds
Response Time: 60 seconds

3. Passage:

Behavior modeling, or observational learning, is a learning process that occurs through observing and imitating others. A model can be a parent, sibling, friend, or teacher, but in childhood, a model is typically someone of authority or higher status. This type of learning is based on observation of the environment and repetition according to the observations made. This type of learning is typically studied in children, and experimentation suggests that children will behave in ways similar to those they have observed. Research has shown that a specific neuron called a mirror neuron has an influential role in this type of learning.

Speaking passage 2: A lecture by a male professor

Practice Audio: Speaking Passage 2: Lecture
Visit mometrix.com/academy and enter Code: 108479

Question: Use the example from the lecture to explain what behavior modeling is and how it works.

Preparation Time: 30 seconds
Response Time: 60 seconds

4. Speaking passage 3: A lecture by a male professor

Practice Audio: Speaking Passage 3: Lecture
Visit mometrix.com/academy and enter Code: 108478

Question: Use information from the lecture to explain the two types of morphemes and how they influence a language's category.

Preparation Time: 20 seconds
Response Time: 60 seconds

Writing

Additional Instructions for the Test

On the TOEFL, you will be given two writing tasks to complete. The first task is the **integrated writing task**, in which you will read a short excerpt from a university-level text and then listen to a lecture corresponding to the text. You must then write a response to a question asking about the main ideas and how the two sources of information relate. Your response should be between 150 and 225 words, although exceeding this amount is acceptable so long as the question is answered effectively. You will have 20 minutes to write your response.

The second writing task is the **independent writing task**, which requires you to answer a question based upon your own personal experience. This may be asking if you agree or disagree with a statement and what reasons you have for thinking so. Your response for the independent writing task should be at least 100 words. You will have 10 minutes to write your response.

Integrated Writing Task

Reading passage: An excerpt from a psychology textbook

Human intelligence is incredibly difficult to define, and many psychologists and scientists have competing opinions. Intelligence is influenced by a variety of characteristics such as behavior, cognition, and emotion, which make intelligence more of a spectrum than a binary. There are typically three categories of ability studied in research about intelligence: problem-solving ability (i.e., logical thinking), verbal ability (i.e., ability to speak clearly and orderly), and practical intelligence (i.e., problem-solving skills).

The most challenging aspect of studying intelligence is measuring it since scientists must devise a thorough approach to investigate all aspects of intellect. Alfred Binet, a French psychologist, was tasked with evaluating children with learning difficulties to see if they were mentally capable of attending traditional schools. He and a psychiatrist named Theodore Simon developed one of the first IQ, or intelligence quotient, tests, called the Binet-Simon test, in response. The questions centered on attention, memory, problem-solving, and perception. The test consisted of 56 tasks and questions arranged in increasing difficulty based on age. A three-year-old, for example, would be asked to repeat sentences and numbers or describe pictures, whereas a 10-year-old would be asked to build sentences. This feature of the test allowed for a comparison of a normal child of any age to be made with the test taker, which was essential for obtaining an accurate measure of intelligence. The test was scored by dividing the child's mental age by his or her physical age and multiplying the result by 100. A 100 on the test meant that the student was of average intelligence, while a score below 100 meant that he or she was of below average intelligence. Even today, many people believe that a higher score correlates with greater intellectual ability.

The Wechsler Intelligence Scale for Children (WISC) was proposed by psychologist David Wechsler in 1949 and is one of the most widely used tests today. This test, too, attempts to quantify a child's intellectual skills but is based on five categories: verbal comprehension, visual-spatial abilities, fluid reasoning, working memory, and processing speed. The WISC is used to diagnose learning disabilities and attention-deficit/hyperactivity disorder, and several studies have touted its effectiveness in predicting the academic behavior of these types of students.

Writing passage 2: A lecture by a female professor

Practice Audio: Writing Passage 1: Lecture
Visit mometrix.com/academy and enter Code: 108477

Question: Summarize the points made in the lecture and explain how they respond to the points in the reading passage.

Independent Writing Task

Your professor is teaching a class on modern media in society and has asked a question on the class message board. Write a response to the professor's question. Your response should be at least 100 words long.

Professor: Over the next few weeks, we'll be talking about the role of film and TV in society. As media has become more dominant in our lives, it has taken on the roles of entertainer, informer, and educator. Specifically, we'll be discussing the role of film and TV as an educator in today's society.

Do you think that film and TV have the responsibility of education? If so, what should producers and directors keep in mind when creating media?

Aadya: I think that TV and film are already educators and not taking responsibility for this role would be negligent. Since we, as a society, are becoming more isolated due to media, many children and adults are socialized using TV and film instead of face-to-face interaction alone. Producers should keep this in mind as they choose what shows and movies will be made and released to the public. While the type of audience member changes based on the media being consumed, producers and directors should consider the kinds of characters they glorify and the types of language as well. If a character is a bully, children may watch and understand that there is glory or power in being a bully.

Suhas: TV shows and films educate their viewers, but this isn't a responsibility that producers and directors have to accommodate unless they are creating media for the purpose of education like documentaries. Most TV shows and films are just to entertain the audiences, and they shouldn't have to take on the responsibility of educating the public if that's not their goal. In comedies and dramas, for example, characters often act in unpredictable or immoral ways for shock factor. Sometimes the characters who commit crimes are the main characters, and the audience ends up hoping they don't get caught. TV and film offer viewers a chance to disconnect from reality, and it's the responsibility of every consumer to educate themselves and not take what they see on TV as truth.

Answer Key and Explanations for Test #2

Reading

Passage 1

1. C: Paragraph 1 explains that activation of defense-related genes contributes to stronger resistance against bacterial infection, production of suberin, and reinforcing of the cell wall. However, there is no indication that the SAR pathway is initiated in response to abiotic (nonliving) factors such as wind. Therefore, the activation of these defense-related genes would not provide the plant with stronger resistance against wind damage.

2. A: Fungi do transfer defense signals to neighboring plants. Paragraph 4 of the passage states that common mycorrhizal networks (CMNs), which are fungal networks, have been shown to pass defense signals from the plants that have initiated them to other plants of the same or different species. (B) The passage states that the fungi select the plant host, not that plants choose fungal hosts. (C) Plants do not benefit from fungi receiving plant sugars. Plants make sugars during photosynthesis, and these sugars are nutrients. When fungi receive these sugars, the plants are not able to use them. (D) The passage does not discuss fungi protecting themselves from bacteria. Furthermore, fungi protecting themselves from bacteria does not describe a way that mycorrhizae benefit plants—the plant would receive no obvious help from this.

3. C: This sentence gives examples of the different gene products used in the SAR pathway and the effects they have in containing the pathogen (cell well rigidification, synthesis of proteins, etc.). Its purpose is to give the reader a concrete idea of what the SAR pathway consists of. (A) Neither the paragraph nor the sentence have mentioned the jasmonic acid pathway by this point in the passage, so it cannot be a comparison. (B) The sentence prior to this one states that the SAR pathway initiates a defense response but does not state anything about using proteins. However, the sentence above states that PR proteins are used in the response. (D) The sentence does not suggest that the salicylic acid pathway is not effective or ineffective. It merely states the defense responses taken.

4. D: This sentence highlights the large percentage of plants that have a fungal symbiont, which emphasizes the importance of mycorrhizal fungi. In the sentence prior to this, the passage states that defense signals may be transferred via mycorrhizal fungi. By then stating that 90 percent of plants have symbiotic fungi, the author is implying that these defenses must be important and provide evolutionary advantages. (A) This sentence does not suggest any drawbacks to fungal symbiosis. In fact, it only states that plants and fungi often exist in symbiosis. In the following sentences, there are only examples of how the fungi benefit the plants. (B) This sentence offers no examples of plants with or without mycorrhizal connections. The sentence states that many plants have connections but does not specify which plants. (C) The sentence does not provide a foundational understanding of defense signals. That information is found in the previous three paragraphs. This sentence is focused on the prevalence and importance of mycorrhizal fungi.

5. B: The passage states that the SAR and ISR defense pathways *confer* resistance to pathogens. The passage also states that the pathways operate against different pathogens, which are infectious bodies. As a result, *confer* must mean a word similar to *give* or *offer* since the pathways allow the plants to defend against the pathogens. The word *grant* means to bestow upon or give, so it is close in meaning to *confer*. (A) *Possess* means to own, (C) *deny* means to not allow, and (D) *converse* means to speak with.

6. D: The passage states that mycorrhizae can be *selective* about their hosts before stating that they only pair with specific plants. This means that the fungi do not pair with just any plant but rather choose which plants they pair with. The word *selective* means choosy or specific in this context, which is only expressed by answer D. (A) *General* means imprecise or inexact, (B) *cautious* means to be careful, and (C) *indiscriminate* means unselective.

7. B: The SAR pathway is used to sequester, or isolate, the pathogen from the plant, which offers resistance and makes the plant less likely to become infected. (A) The sentence does not state that the infection will not reach other plants in the vicinity. (C) The plants do not perish quickly. They are resistant to pathogens and more likely to live. (D) While this is likely true, it is not mentioned in the sentence and is, therefore, not a good summary.

8. A: The sentence states that scientists have hypothesized that plants may be able to use volatile organic compounds (VOCs), which are airborne compounds, to initiate the defense pathways in their neighbors. (B) These compounds do not elicit defense responses in pathogens but in plants. (C) Plants do not trigger defense responses in VOCs but in other plants by using VOCs. (D) The sentence does not talk about toxins interacting with plants but pathogens and VOCs, which may elicit defense responses.

9. B: The missing sentence belongs in place [2] because it includes the word *therefore*, which means that it is making a conclusion based on information in the previous sentence. In this case, the sentence before the missing sentence must explain that certain plants cannot accumulate salicylic acid. The only sentence that provides this explanation is the first sentence, which means that the new sentence must be directly after it in place [2].

10. A, B, **and** D: Paragraph 4 states the importance of mycorrhizae in transferring chemical signals and nutrients. Paragraphs 1 and 2 discuss the different biological mechanisms plants have to help them fight off pathogens. Paragraph 3 expresses that plants can influence their neighbors to initiate defensive pathways. (C) This is sometimes true, but VOCs do influence other plants when they are in close proximity. (E) There are plants that can use both the SAR and ISR pathways even though some plants can only employ one pathway. (F) Fungi do only connect with specific plants, but this does not negatively affect the environment.

Passage 2

11. D: The theory of phrenology was based on the idea that different areas of the brain are responsible for specific personality traits, which is a form of specialization. According to this theory, the development of these personality traits in the brain affects the skull by pushing it outward. Thus, the brain affects the development of the skull, and scientists can predict human behavior based on its analysis. Gall was only correct in describing the specialization in the brain because the left and right hemispheres do largely control certain abilities like language and spatial reasoning. (A) The brain does not grow outward. (B) The brain does not affect the development of the skull. (C) Scientists cannot predict behavior based on the structure of the skull because the brain has no influence on the skull's development.

12. A: Wernicke and Broca both treated patients with aphasia—an inability to speak or understand spoken and/or written words. When the patients were autopsied, they were found to have damage to the left hemisphere, although in slightly different areas; the patients showed different symptoms. Wernicke and Broca both hypothesized that the "seat" of language was located in the left hemisphere. (B) Wernicke's and Broca's theories suggested that because language was controlled by the left hemisphere, only damage to the left side of the brain would impact language function. (C) The only way Wernicke and Broca could analyze brain damage was through autopsy, but their theories were not based on the importance of autopsy. In fact, the author states that neurologists today are more easily able to study brain damage on a living patient, which allows for deeper understanding. (D) Wernicke's and Broca's theories were that only the left hemisphere was responsible for language function because their patients had brain damage on the left side.

13. B: The sentence states that scientists in the past had to wait years for a patient to die of natural causes in order to understand his or her brain functionality and damage. The next sentence in the passage then states that now it is easier to study brain damage because scientists can study a living patient. Thus, this waiting period was a scientific obstacle. (A) This is incorrect because the sentence does not contrast Wernicke's and Broca's methods. In fact, this paragraph implies a similarity in their research—they both had to wait a long time to study their patients. (C) The sentence does not disprove the assertion that technological invention is necessary for science because it does not mention technological development. Scientists at this time still used technological tools to discover more about their patients. The sentence instead sets up a recognition of the importance of technology in the scientific fields because further developments have made research easier. (D) The sentence does not suggest that scientists are still struggling to understand brain function because it does not mention the present nor brain function. Paragraph 5 discusses the lack of data in understanding brain function, but paragraph 4 is mainly about how neurological research has changed over time.

14. C: The sentence shows an example of the left hemisphere's functionality by explaining the effect of damage to that side of the brain. When the left hemisphere is damaged, patients have difficulty with word recognition and communication with others, thus giving an example of how the left hemisphere controls language-related function. (A) The sentence does not prove that the left hemisphere has little effect on language function; it proves the opposite. The left hemisphere has great control over language function because when it is damaged, patients struggle with understanding language. (B) This sentence does not state a difference between Broca's and Wernicke's discoveries but instead highlights a similarity. Both scientists discovered that damage to the left hemisphere resulted in their patients having difficulty with language-related function. They both came to the conclusion that the center of language control in the brain is in the left hemisphere. (D) While this sentence gives examples of how the left hemisphere controls language function, the previous two sentences in the passage clearly show that this is not its only responsibility. The left hemisphere is responsible for fine motor control, reasoning, problem-solving, and interpretation.

15. D: The word *corroborate* means to confirm or support. In the sentence, the author states that Gall collected skulls and calculated their cranial protuberances in order to *corroborate*, or support, his theories. The word can be understood because Gall studied skulls to understand their qualities, so he would be trying to prove his beliefs by analyzing more skulls. (A) To *publicize* means to spread information or make widely known. The sentence does not discuss whether Gall spread his beliefs or publicized them at all; instead, it focuses on his studies. (B) To *contradict* means to disagree or to oppose. Gall did not seek to disprove his own theories but to prove them. This can be understood by the fact that he collected data (i.e., skulls) to prove his theories. (C) To *understand* means to comprehend, which would not make sense because the person who founds a study would already understand his or her own beliefs.

16. B: The word *impaired* means to be damaged or obstructed. In this case, *damaged* is the appropriate word choice because it means to be weakened or hurt. The sentence describes how a wound had *impaired* the patient's frontal lobe in his brain's left hemisphere, which made him unable to express himself verbally. In this case, *damage* makes sense because the writer mentions a wound and a lack of capability. (A) *Dissected* means to cut or take apart, often in a scientific setting.

While the scientists dissected the brain during the autopsy, a wound does not dissect the brain. Furthermore, this word does not show that the capabilities of the patient were hindered. (C) *Dulled* means to be less intense or reduced. This word does not make sense in context because the patient's linguistic function was not diminished but entirely absent. Furthermore, a wound does not dull; it damages. (D) *Encouraged* means to give support or stimulate something new. In this case, the wound did not support or stimulate the brain but instead damaged it entirely.

17. C: The original sentence states that under phrenology, the brain was divided into regions (i.e., separated into different sections), each of which was thought to control a particular personality trait. The size of a skull's bump in that section was thus directly related to how prominent a personality trait was. This is the only correct answer because it states that sections of the brain control personality traits that can be measured based on the skull's bumps. (A) This is incorrect because a person with a large bump will not have a more interesting personality but a more developed specific personality trait based on what region the bump is in. (B) While this answer may have some truth, the original sentence does not mention autopsies, and the word *divide* is meant to suggest a figurative meaning—not to cut but to be delineated into a map or regions. (D) The sentence does not suggest that the brain is not whole; instead, it is mapped to have different regions that each control a single personality trait, not several.

18. A: The sentence states that although there is no proof, and little evidence, many scientists believe that the two hemispheres are responsible for different functions, which leads to the development of certain skills, also known as hemispheric specialization. This answer states that the two parts of the brain are responsible for different tasks and the development of skills, noting that there is no proof. (B) The sentence specifically states that the hemispheres are responsible for different tasks and skills, not the same. Therefore, the halves are not analogous. (C) The sentence does not mention the size of the hemispheres or suggest dominance of one hemisphere over the other. The brain does not favor a side because, although the two have separate specialties, they largely work together. (D) There is actually little evidence that suggests that the hemispheres are dedicated to different tasks and skill development. While there is evidence in support of functional asymmetry and specialization in the brain, there is little data to suggest that this leads to skills development. However, many scientists believe and study this theory.

19. B: The first sentence introduces the corpus callosum, a set of nerve fibers that connects the hemispheres. The sentence to be added references the corpus callosum. Therefore, the correct answer cannot be (A) because the added sentence would reference the corpus callosum before its introduction. (B) This is correct because the sentence referencing the corpus callosum should be directly after the sentence where it is first mentioned. Furthermore, the added sentence offers a transition between the first and second sentence. It states that the corpus callosum connects the hemispheres despite their distinctions, which leads into the second sentence, which discusses partial functional asymmetry. (C) This answer along with (D) do not make sense because the author has transitioned to a new topic of discussion. The second and third sentences are no longer referencing the connection between the two hemispheres but the differences between their specialties. Thus, the added sentence would be too far away from the definition of the corpus callosum.

20. A, D, and E: (A) As stated in paragraph 1, phrenology was the study of personality traits, or psychological characteristics, based on skull, or cranial, shape. Phrenologists would analyze the skull with their fingers and measuring tapes to discern bumps and ridges in the skull to determine personality traits. This is a main idea because the first two paragraphs explain phrenology. (D) Scientists discovered that the capacity for language is controlled by certain parts of the brain. Broca and Wernicke both studied the brains of patients who had had difficulty speaking and understanding language and discovered that the patients' brains had damage in the left hemisphere. This led both scientists to the conclusion that the "seat" of language is in the left hemisphere. However, more studies have shown that while the left hemisphere houses language function, it does not alone solely control this activity. The left and right brain more frequently work together instead of separately. (E) Developments in science have made it easier to study the brain's function. As stated in paragraph 4, it was very difficult to study the brain before modern inventions because scientists had to wait for a patient to die of natural causes. The advent of neuroimaging, among other tools, has allowed scientists to study the brain on living patients, deepening the level of study possible and leading to more discoveries. (B) The left hemisphere controls language function including semantics and grammar, along with analytical reasoning, problem-solving, and interpretive ability as stated in paragraph 6. The right hemisphere controls emotion, perception, and spatial orientation. (C) Phrenology was a pseudoscientific study that has been widely rejected aside from the idea that the brain has specialized areas. A person's personality traits cannot be measured based on skull ridges. (F) While the left and right hemispheres do work together, they have different functions and specializations. The left hemisphere is primarily centered around language, while the right is concerned with socio-emotionality.

Listening

1. B: The main topic of the lecture is the complicated psychology of the character Lady Macbeth in Shakespeare's play *Macbeth.* Choices A and C are mentioned, but they are details of the lecture rather than the central point. Choice D is not explicitly mentioned in the lecture, so it is also incorrect.

2. D: When the professor says, "I can see I'm losing some of you," she is implying that her students are not focusing on the lecture; in other words, they are losing interest in the lecture and are distracted by other thoughts. In this case, the professor believes that this is because the students are worried about their exam grades. She says: "I can see I'm losing some of you because I bet many of you have your minds on last week's midterm, so let's end our discussion here today and go over your test..." The other answer choices do not correctly explain this figure of speech.

3. B: Questions that are posed during lectures but are not given a pause to receive actual answers are called *rhetorical questions*. This is a device used to help strengthen one's argument by engaging listeners and tasking them to examine their own thoughts as they consider the argument. The professor employs this device when she asks, "Do you guys see how the key to Lady Macbeth's strategy for gaining influence over her husband is to somewhat switch the gender roles within her marriage?"

4. B: The professor argues that the strength of Shakespeare's plays and a quality that made him a great playwright is the fact that his works consider the complexities of human nature through character development. At the beginning of the lecture, she says: "As we've been discussing, one element of Shakespeare's writing that sets him apart from his predecessors, and arguably made him a great playwright, was his ability to create characters with intricate and interesting psychologies ... These complexities um ... evoke his audience's sympathies, and subsequently heightens their interest in the play." Choice A is a true statement, but it doesn't answer *why* he is considered a great playwright. While some of his characters (such as Lady Macbeth) are deviant according to the standards of the time, Shakespeare's plays don't necessarily *persuade* audience members to be deviant, so Choice C is incorrect. Choice D is not really mentioned in the lecture; while specific characters and kings are named, this is not emphasized as Shakespeare's lasting literary impact.

5. C: The professor argues that Shakespeare's characters were complex and Lady Macbeth is no exception. Therefore, she would likely think that Lady Macbeth is character who is realistic in her psychological complexities. She mentions that one of Shakespeare's strengths as a playwright was the development of characters with "intricate and interesting psychologies." As she explains: "Many of Shakespeare's main characters are written in general compliance with 'good' and 'evil' archetypes, but just like generally 'good' and 'evil' people in real life, the motives of his characters are complex."

6. A: The lecture is mostly about Lady Macbeth, but her husband, Macbeth, is described with words like "passive," and he is compared to a scared (frightened) child. The professor says that "Macbeth's ambition has been purposefully implanted by his wife" and that he "submits to his wife's leadership," indicating that she thinks that Macbeth would not have murdered the king on his own. The contrast between the complex character of Lady Macbeth and her husband implies that Macbeth is a simple character and that he serves mostly to do what Lady Macbeth wants.

7. B: The professor asks the student if she is there to see her to talk about an independent study, and the student replies "yes" at the beginning of the conversation. (A) The student does not ask why there are no advanced Italian classes. She brings up the fact that there is nothing above intermediate this year. The professor then acknowledges that the professor for advanced Italian stepped down, and it is clear that the student already knew this. (C) The student does not say that she has done any previous translation work. She just says she has one or two stories picked out already that she wants to work on, but she needs more suggestions. (D) The student is applying for credits based on the independent study, so the credits are not the main purpose of the conversation. She is mainly there to talk about the requirements for the independent study, so the topic of credits for the study comes up.

8. C: The professor mentions that the previous advanced Italian professor transferred positions by saying that she had to "step down" and that her "new job is going well." (A) There is no mention of the Italian department losing funding. Instead, it is stated that the previous advanced Italian professor stepped down to take a new job. (B) There is no indication that too few people signed up to take the class as it is not mentioned in the conversation. Instead, the previous professor is noted to have left her position for a different job. (D) Neither person mentions that the previous Italian professor received complaints about her teaching. Instead, the student says that the previous professor "really got [her] excited about language study."

9. D: The student states in the conversation that she would like "to do a translated collection of several short stories." (A) The student does not want to do a literature review of translated texts because she wants to translate the stories herself. A literature review requires reading and analysis of texts, but this student would like to do the translation rather than an analysis. (B) The student does not mention doing fieldwork with translators at work. Instead, she talks about translating texts herself—ones that have never been translated before. (C) The student stated in the conversation that she does not want to translate texts that have been previously translated. She does say that retranslation is "interesting" but that she wants "to focus on more obscure texts."

10. A and C: The professor states that "the amount of work will depend on the text ... and how difficult it is to translate." Therefore, (A) must be correct because it states that the amount of work for each meeting depends on the text's difficulty. (C) The professor also states that their weekly meetings will be focused on the student's progress. She states that they will "have a meeting once a week to discuss the work that you've done outside of our meeting times." She also states that the student should come to meetings prepared to talk about and present her work for at least an hour. In this case, it is understood that the student's progress in her translation will be the main, if not the only, topic of their meetings. (B) The student is applying for three credits (not five) because there is a choice. The professor tells the student that the expectation for work depends on how many credits she applies for. The student then says she is "thinking about applying for three credits." (D) The weekly meetings will last for one hour, not half an hour. The teacher states that the student should come to their meetings "prepared to talk about and present [her] work for at least an hour."

11. D: The student has mentioned that she doesn't want to work on popular texts in the story because she wants to focus on obscure texts. The professor responds with this statement. In this case, "worked to death" means that the *Divine Comedy* has been overstudied. Since the text's popularity and previous translations have been stated, the listener can infer that the book is widely studied. This implies that the text is overstudied for the purposes of the student's work. (A) The professor does not suggest that this text has lost its meaning. The *Divine Comedy* is overstudied, but that does not mean that it has become unimportant. (B) The professor does not imply a misinterpretation of the *Divine Comedy* in earlier translations. She simply emphasizes that a large amount of scholarship has been directed toward this text. (C) The student states that retranslation is interesting, but the professor's statement does not reinforce that statement. Instead, the professor states that the *Divine Comedy* has been overstudied.

12. B: This lesson is mostly about autosomal dominant inheritance since the lecture mainly focuses on this topic. The professor explains the definitions of the words *autosomal* and *dominant* and provides examples of how these disorders operate within the general population (brown eyes and Huntington's disease). (A) While the professor mentions the transmission rate of genetic diseases, she talks about it in reference to autosomal dominant disorders. The majority of the lesson is not about transmission rates. (C) Most of the lesson is not about different heritable diseases. The professor uses the examples provided to illustrate the way that autosomal dominant disorders are inherited. (D) The professor briefly mentions sex-linked traits but does not spend much time elaborating on them. As a result, sex-linked traits are not the main idea of the lecture.

13. A and C: (A) This is correct because the professor explains how two copies of the disease alleles of a gene, one from each parent, are necessary for a person to have a recessive disorder. In this case, one parent would have the disease, and the other would have one copy of the allele, meaning that a child could inherit the disease. (C) The same is true for this answer. If both parents have the disorder, the child will also have the disorder because he or she would inherit two recessive alleles, which are necessary for recessive trait expression. (B) This is not possible because two copies of a recessive allele must be present for a recessive trait to be expressed. Both of the parents must pass the recessive allele to the child, but if one parent is not a carrier, he or she cannot pass on the required copy. Thus, the child cannot inherit the disease. (D) The same is true of a carrier parent and an unaffected parent. If a parent is a carrier, he or she has only one copy of the recessive allele that can be passed on. However, an unaffected person has zero copies of that allele, meaning it cannot be passed on to the child.

14. D: The professor illustrates that dominant traits override recessive traits with the example of blue and brown eyes. She states that when one allele for brown eyes is present, the child will have brown eyes. This happens because the allele for brown eyes is dominant to (i.e., overpowers) the allele for blue eyes. The teacher explained this concept so the students could understand how dominant traits take precedence over recessive traits. (A) Recessive traits are expressed when the person has two copies of the allele, not one. The professor explains this by stating that dominant traits are expressed based on only one allele. (B) Two copies of the brown eye allele are not necessary for its inheritance because it is a dominant gene. In this case, only one allele is required because it will overpower a recessive allele in its expression. (C) The professor does not state that brown eyes are more common than blue eyes, so it cannot be a part of the illustration. While it would be a good inference to make from the information we have, it is not mentioned in the lecture.

15. C: The professor mentions Huntington's disease to show how autosomal disorders work in the general population and to give an example of a dominant disorder. She explains how only one copy of the allele of this disease is necessary and how it exists in the population. (A) None of the students said something incorrect about dominant disorders; the professor instead introduces the topic to round out the discussion of autosomal dominant inheritance. (B) None of the students asked a question about Huntington's disease, so the professor mentioned it to further elaborate on dominant disorders. (D) The professor had not previously mentioned a recessive disorder. Furthermore, the professor does not compare and contrast Huntington's disease with a recessive disorder.

16. C: People who have genetic diseases often choose to not have children because they do not want to pass the disease onto their children. However, people often don't know they have Huntington's disease until later in their life. The professor states that symptoms usually appear around ages 30 to 50, and many people have already had children at this point. As a result, the disease is passed to the next generation. (A) People with Huntington's disease do present symptoms; the disease is neurodegenerative, so symptoms get worse over time starting in adulthood. (B) Huntington's disease is a dominant disorder, meaning that people have the disease even if they have just one copy of the disease allele. Children are less likely to have recessive genetic diseases because two copies of the disease allele are necessary for the disease to be expressed. (D) The professor did not state that people with Huntington's disease rarely live past 50 years old. She said that they do not show symptoms until they are 30 to 50 years old and did not say how long they live after they show symptoms.

17. D: To continue the lesson, the professor is drawing a comparison between dominant and recessive disorders. She does this by asking questions about recessive disorders after discussing dominant disorders in detail. Since she just explained how autosomal dominant disorders present in the population, she draws a comparison between dominant and recessive disorders. (A) The professor wants her students to think about the questions she is asking, but she doesn't say that they should already know this information. Instead, she wants them to think about the answers to the questions and make educated guesses. (B) The professor has not yet discussed autosomal recessive disorders in detail, so she cannot be reminding students of an earlier lecture. Instead, she is transitioning to the next topic by asking the students to consider the similarities and differences between recessive and dominant disorders. (C) The professor has not made a mistake in this lecture, and she does not try to correct anything either. If she were correcting herself, she would likely apologize and explain the flaw in her logic.

18. B: This lecture is mainly about classical conditioning. The professor spends most of his time discussing its principles, including that of learning and the process of conditioning. He discusses examples of classical conditioning: a child being frightened by a dog, Pavlov's dogs, and food poisoning. (A) While the professor mentions operant conditioning and modeling, the majority of the lecture is focused on classical conditioning. Because he does not discuss the differences or give examples of operant conditioning, the lecture cannot be mostly about the differences between the two conditioning types. (C) The professor does talk about the definition of learning, but he does not discuss more than one definition. He only mentions the behaviorist definition of learning. (D) The lesson is not mostly about the way behavior changes over time. It is about the concept of classical conditioning. While behavior does change in classical conditioning, the point of the lecture was not about the change; it was about classifying this behavior change as a certain kind of learning.

19. A: The professor states that behaviorists believed learning to be a behavioral change that resulted from an experience in the environment. For example, Pavlov's dogs associated the sound of a bell with the presentation of food, which resulted in a reaction to the bell without the presentation of food. Thus, the dogs learned that the bell was indicative of food and changed their behavior as a result. (B) The professor describes behaviorist learning as a behavioral change in response to the environment; however, learning is not an innate ability to experience information because it requires a behavioral change. Experiencing information is not learning. (C) The behaviorist definition of learning requires that the learning is subconscious, meaning that the individual learning does not know that he or she is learning. The person does not knowingly change his or her behavior. (D) Learning also cannot be defined as an automatic response because the response is something that must first be learned. While learning does occur in response to external stimuli, it is not an automatic response. The response must first be learned in order to become automatic.

20. C: In classical conditioning, the learner is often completely unaware of his or her behavioral change. In the example of food poisoning, the professor mentions that a person may associate being ill with what he or she ate last; however, this is not a choice made by the individual but a subconscious reaction to the environment. A person does not choose to be sick in response to eating that same thing. (A) In classical conditioning, a neutral stimulus like Pavlov's bell is associated with the stimulus of presented food. (B) The learned reaction becomes automatic after it is learned. Once the dogs had associated the bell with the presentation of food, they could not choose whether to salivate. It simply happened automatically. (D) Pavlov's dogs learned to salivate at the sound of a bell via classical conditioning because this learning involved the association of a neutral stimulus with another stimulus, and the response after learning was automatic.

21. D: The professor describes how a child may hear a barking dog and become frightened. As a result, the child will be frightened every time he or she sees a dog. This is an example of classical conditioning because the child associates a neutral stimulus (the dog) with fear subconsciously. The professor discusses how this illustrates the principle of learning as described by behaviorists. (A) The example of the child and barking dog does not explain how Pavlov trained his dogs because the example of the dog barking and frightening the child is not a controlled experiment. No one was repeatedly exposing a child to frightening animals like Pavlov did with his dogs and food. (B) This example does not compare how children and animals learn because classical conditioning can occur with individuals of any age or species. The purpose of the example is to show how classical conditioning can occur in an uncontrolled environment. (C) While this example does show how fear can lead to avoidance in children, the main point is not to specify children's responses, fear, or avoidance. Instead, the example is meant to illustrate the process of a learned response based on two associated stimuli.

22. A: The dogs responded to the sound of the bell because Pavlov presented food to the dogs only after ringing the bell. Therefore, the dogs learned to associate the sound of the bell with food to the point that the sound alone could produce a response. (B) The dogs did not previously have a response to the sound of a bell until Pavlov trained them; therefore, the dogs could not have already had a response. The response had to be conditioned by the association of the bell with food. (C) While the sound of a bell may have caught the dogs' attention, the main point of the bell was to associate a response to the bell based on the presentation of food. Then, when the dogs had learned the association, they would respond with salivation to the sound of the bell even without food. (D) Even though the dogs salivated when the bell was rung, they did not actively choose to salivate. It was an automatic response that occurred because an association had been made between the bell and the presentation of food.

23. C: When the teacher says, "That's close," what he means is that the student almost had the right answer but that it was incomplete. This can be understood because the teacher goes on to elaborate on the student's response by stating that learning is also a behavioral change based on an interaction with the environment. (A) The student is not encouraged to continue her response—she has finished talking. Instead, the professor indicates that her answer was not entirely correct. (B) The professor does not ask the student to correct herself but corrects her instead. The student does not speak again after this interaction. (D) The student does not give a complete response, so it seems that she does not completely understand the answer. Instead, she is missing a key component of learning, which is to change behavior after an experience in the environment. The student only mentioned that learning is the environmental experience.

24. B: The professor wanted to speak to the student to commend (compliment) her for her work in class. The professor says that she "scored the highest grade in the class" and states that her lab drawings were very detailed. This reason is why the professor initially calls her over. (A) The student does not have any issues with her classwork. Instead, the professor explains that her lab journal was the best in the class. (C) The professor does not give the student instructions on how to complete the final project. While the student does ask a question about the project, it is not the main reason why the professor asks her to speak with him. (D) The professor offers the student an internship opportunity, but that is not the initial reason he asks to speak with her. He first calls her over to speak with her about her lab reports. Then, after they have spoken about the final project, he discusses an internship opportunity.

25. B: The professor states that the student's lab journal "was nearly 60 pages long, and the drawings were very detailed." Based on this statement, it is clear that the drawings and notes in the student's lab journal were very detailed. (A) The student did not include unique specimen drawings as that would mean that she had drawn different plants than everyone else in the class. Instead, the professor describes the drawings as detailed and implies that the notes are detailed as well by mentioning the page count. (C) The student did not turn in her lab journal early. She does state that she wants to finish the final project early, but this project is not the same as the lab journal, which has already been turned in. (D) While the professor does praise the student for her detailed lab drawings, he does not mention an illustration on the front. Instead, he focuses on the drawings of the specimens within the lab journal, stating how detailed they are.

26. A: The student mentions that the lab door wouldn't open for some of her classmates while discussing the final project. The professor responds that the students should be able to open it with their student IDs. He also states that if the IDs don't work, the students should contact a security guard to help them. In this case, the professor is offering a solution to the problem of the lab doors not opening. (B) The professor does not remind the student about the security guard's responsibilities. Instead, he states that a guard should be able to help with a certain problem. If he had reminded the student about the guard's responsibilities, he likely would have listed them or discussed keeping the campus safe, which is not included in this conversation. (C) The student has no behavior problems. The professor has complimented her work, and he is trying to solve a problem related to the final project. Because the lab doors won't open, he recommends that students contact a security guard to help. (D) The security guard is not the reason that the problem is occurring. Instead, the guard is the solution. The cause of the problem is that the doors aren't opening on weekends, so the students cannot work on their final projects. The security guard is able to open the doors, thus providing a solution.

27. C and D: While discussing the internship, the professor asks if the student would be interested in working for the town's herbarium. He states that the student would mostly be preparing DNA samples and performing DNA analyses along with caring for the specimens. (A) While the professor states that the student will be caring for the specimens, he does not mention cataloging them. Cataloging implies labeling or numbering, which is not brought up in this conversation. (B) While the professor states that the student will be performing DNA analyses, he mentions that his colleague is looking for interns "to pick up some of the testing." In this case, the student would not be conducting experiments but, more likely, performing routine testing procedures using the lab equipment.

28. D: The professor says this to transition to talk about a summer internship opportunity. This can be inferred because, directly after asking this question, he brings up the internship at the herbarium. He likely wanted to know if the student was going to be around and able to work in the herbarium before offering the work. When the student states that she will be in the city, he asks if she is interested in the internship. (A) The student's final project has not yet been turned in. In this case, it would not make sense for the professor to be asking her to correct work that he has not seen. (B) The professor does not mention the student's studies over the summer. Instead, he transitions into offering her an internship. (C) The professor does not mention any travel plans or recommendations for the student. Instead, he offers her an internship opportunity.

Speaking

1. Sample response: Standardized tests not being the best way to see if you are ready for college for three reasons. First, standardized tests only, uh, are about some classes, but in college, you need to have different abilities like problem-solving or critical thinking. Second reason is that standardized tests only test you at one time. You may be very smart but had a bad day or was distracted while taking the test. You may still do well in college despite a lower score. Moving on, standardized tests don't test if you are able to handle college stress outside of school. They, uh, don't ask about things like talking to people or making decisions, so standardized tests are just, uh, not the best way to see if you are ready.

Explanation of sample response scoring: The response is at a high level and would score a 3 out of 4. This speaker provided a full response with a clearly stated opinion and three different, developed reasons. However, there are some grammatical errors. The first sentence includes an incorrect verb tense, which should read: "Standardized tests are not the best way." The third sentence should read: "The second reason is." The fourth sentence should read: "You may be ... or were distracted." Despite these errors, the response is still comprehensible. The speaker also struggles with clarity at the end of the response, which states that standardized tests are not the best way to see if you are ready but does not say what you should be ready for.

2. Sample response: The, uh, school makes the announcement that students, uh, that the library will be closed more because the librarian is not the librarian anymore. The man said that he did not like this because the people who don't have Wi-Fi or internet can't have it at their homes. So, the library gives Wi-Fi, and these people can't do their work. The second reason is that people who work in the day don't have time go the library to get books. The third reason is that people who writing essays can't get the books for essays because the library is not open.

Explanation of sample response scoring: This response would score a 2 out of 4 on the exam. The speaker mentions several of the main points in the conversation but does not clearly state them all. For example, the speaker states, "So, the library gives Wi-Fi, and these people can't do their work." This statement is not fully comprehensible as the listener doesn't understand if the library having Wi-Fi is a problem or how it relates to people not being able to do their work. A better sentence would be, "The library has Wi-Fi, which means that people can't do their work if it closes early." Furthermore, this speaker reuses vocabulary to express ideas. In the first sentence, the speaker states that the school announces that the library is closed because "the librarian is not the librarian anymore." While correct, the speaker could have used the vocabulary from the written text or conversation like "stepped down." The second and third reasons in this response are well explained but still contain grammatical errors like "have time go the library" and "people who writing." These mistakes do not impede understanding, but they do lower the score.

3. Sample response: Behavior modeling happens when people copy the behaviors of other people that they have seen. This is in the lecture because the lecture is about an example of children learning to copy someone's behaviors. The professors says that when ... that there were three groups of kids, and they had to see people, uh, play with a toy. When the people—when the children saw people play with the toy in an aggressive way, they were also aggressive to the toy. But when the children did not see someone play with the toy in an aggressive way, they were not aggressive to the toy. This shows that children can learn how to do things based on watching other people do them first.

Explanation of sample response scoring: This response would score a 4 out of 4. While the speaker does have some awkward phrasing (for example, "people copy the behaviors of other people that they have seen," "This is in the lecture because"), the response is overall coherent and well-structured. The speaker includes the definition of *behavior modeling* and describes it well. The speaker also brings in the example mentioned in the lecture. The speaker does leave out some information about the experiment but focuses on the most important details (namely the aggressive responses in the children who observed aggressive adults), which effectively demonstrate the point. At times, the vocabulary can be a bit repetitive, but the understanding of the response is not impeded, leading to this speaker scoring highly.

4. Sample response: In the lecture, the professor says that there are, uh, two types of morphemes. These are called lexical and grammatical. A lexical morpheme is the meaning of a word. A grammatical morpheme says something like how many of the word there are. For example, the word "dogs" has two morphemes. The word "dog" is a lexical morpheme because it says the meaning, and the "s" is a grammatical morpheme because it says how many. Morphemes can help with languages' categories because they are different in languages, so there are categories. Some languages have a lot of morphemes that are like words, but some other languages have lots of, uh, have—don't have many words but have lots of morphemes in the words.

Explanation of sample response scoring: This response would score a 4 out of 4. The speaker responds to both parts of the question and explains his or her reasoning very well. There are some grammatical issues and repetition towards the end, but the speaker uses the vocabulary presented in the lecture to explain the concept. For example, the definitions of lexical and grammatical morphemes are descriptive, and the speaker uses an example from the lecture to support the descriptions. The speaker's recounting of language categories is an excellent summary of the ways that morphemes influence these categories. The speaker's description of grammatical morphemes, "says something like how many of the word there are," is an incomplete definition but a clear example of a grammatical morpheme. The explanation of language categories is a bit hesitant, but the speaker still explains how morphemes decide language categories, and the examples tie the response together.

Writing

INTEGRATED WRITING TASK

Sample response: The professor begins her lecture with a criticism on IQ tests. Her first argument is that she believes IQ tests are not accurate because they cannot last a lifetime. She says that the people who make IQ tests have to choose different topics to test on, which means they dont actually measure human intelligence completely. They only measure certain parts of it. The reading talks about different kinds of IQ tests. For example, it talks about Alfred Binet who developed the Simon-Binet test. The reading says that his test was used to identify children who were having intellectual problems based on their ability to answer questions and do tasks. But the professor says that Binet said that his IQ test was not made to put a number on human intelligence. Instead, he was trying to help students who were already struggling.

Her second point is that IQ tests are not made for every type of person. She says that many IQ tests are biased towards one race like the WISC test. The reading passage says that the WISC predicts how well children will do in school, but the professor says that many people have said the test is not fair for everyone. The professor says that when developers tried to fix the problem with the test, it created even more problems. This test can help predict how people will do in school, but it is not fairly made.

Lastly, the professor talks about Gardner's theory of multiple intelligence. The reading passage says that there are three categories of intelligence. The professor says that Gardner's theory says that there are eight kinds of intelligence, and she says that most IQ tests dont include them. The professor says that Gardner was trying to make an intelligence scale that was not biased towards one race, so he focused on important types of intelligence for humanity. The professor says that IQ tests are widely used, but they are not always fair because they don't think about all the ways a person can be smart or how someone's race can effect them.

Explanation of sample response scoring: This response would score a 4 out of 5 on the test. The writing is well organized into three separate points made in the lecture, and the writer connects the information in the passage with that in the lecture very well. The professor was giving a lecture on the drawbacks of IQ tests, and the student appropriately recognized the main two critiques and the alternative theory. The first critique was that IQ tests only judge certain aspects of human intelligence, to which the student wrote, "they dont actually measure human intelligence completely." The student supported this assertion with evidence about Alfred Binet stating that his test was not made to measure IQ but to identify children who were struggling academically. The second point in the lecture was that IQ tests are often racially biased, to which the student wrote, "many IQ tests are biased towards one race." To support this point, the student mentioned the WISC and the unhelpful changes made to it. Last, the student mentions Gardner's theory of multiple intelligences, which the professor used as an alternative theory to IQ tests. The student writes about how this theory is less culturally biased and takes into account more aspects of human intelligence. There are some errors made like "dont," "theory of multiple intelligence," and "can effect them," but these do not interfere with comprehension. The student does employ some sophisticated vocabulary but also falls back on specific phrases and sentence structure like "she says" and "the professor says," which could lower the student's score.

INDEPENDENT WRITING TASK

Sample response: In my opinion, TV and film have the responsibility to educate their audiences but only sometimes. As Aadya said, many children grow up watching TV and film. Exposure to bad influences or immoral content could affect them negatively, but Suhas also has a point. TV shows and movies are often meant only as entertainment. However, I don't think that this fact changes the responsibility of producers and directors. Even though TV programs and films are meant to entertain, they have a lot of influence over society. The main goal of TV and film does not have to be education, but viewers shouldn't have to disconnect from their sense of right and wrong while watching media.

Explanation of sample response scoring: This response would likely score a 5 out of 5 on the test. The writing is incredibly clear with few mistakes, none of which impact clarity. Furthermore, the ideas expressed in the writing are quite complex. The writer does not simply summarize the main points of the other students' posts but combines them to form a more interesting response. A restatement of another student's work would not contribute to the discussion and would score much lower. This response, however, uses Suhas's point to explain how media is often used as simple entertainment. It also uses Aadya's post to say that media should have sense of responsibility in portraying messages of right and wrong. Combining the two opinions shows that the writer has a complex understanding of the subject and a well-developed opinion. The vocabulary, too, is varied, which makes the writer sound more professional. While some phrases are a bit simple in form, the work is well-structured and well-written.

Transcripts of Recordings for Test #2

Listening Passage 1: Lecture Transcript

Narrator: Listen to the lecture in a literature class and then answer the questions.

Female professor: As we've been discussing, one element of Shakespeare's writing that sets him apart from his predecessors, and arguably made him a great playwright, was his ability to create characters with intricate and interesting psychologies. Many of Shakespeare's main characters are written in general compliance with "good" and "evil" archetypes, but just like generally "good" and "evil" people in real life, the motives of his characters are complex. These complexities um...evoke his audiences' sympathies, and subsequently heightens their interest in the play. Shakespeare's most famous characters are those that do not conform absolutely to typical protagonist and antagonist roles. These characters prevent audiences from considering and appreciating the play on strictly superficial levels.

So, now that we've had to chance to finish Macbeth, I think you'll see how Shakespeare's portrayal of Lady Macbeth contains these additional dimensions that make her character realistic and engaging. In public, she recognizes and behaves within her social limitations and expectations as a woman, but violates those boundaries while alone or with her husband. Lady Macbeth shifts between the passive role of a wife, the aggressive attitude of a leader, and the tempting behaviors of I don't know...a seductress, in order to advance her and her husband's social and financial status.

Lady Macbeth reveals her scheming and violent nature within her first few lines of the play. She is completely aware that she and her husband have common goals, but that without her influence, Macbeth himself lacks the primal instinct needed to commit the murder of King Duncan. Macbeth's horrible vision of murder is not his own, his ambition has been purposefully implanted by his wife. Macbeth's is extremely passive, and speaks in a tone much like that of a scared child; he asks his wife if they are going to be suspected of the murders. Essentially, the moment that Macbeth submits to his wife's leadership is the moment that the traditional marital and gender roles are reversed.

Do you guys see how the key to Lady Macbeth's strategy for gaining influence over her husband is to somewhat switch the gender roles within her marriage? Just before Macbeth arrives home, Lady Macbeth pleads "unsex me here." So, essentially, Lady Macbeth seeks to lose her female restrictions in order to gain total control over the situation, or...uh...what she sees as her opportunity to gain power over her husband. Lady Macbeth successfully "unsexes" herself by assuming the male role and aggressively taking matters into her own hands throughout the play. Lady Macbeth adjusts her language and tone to make herself more masculine in these instances, which intimidate Macbeth's actions in turn.

In order to avoid suspicion, Lady Macbeth alters her behavior for the public eye as well. She knows that self-effacement and politeness are necessary behaviors to adopt so that she and her husband are able to climb social and financial ladders. The tone of her speech as she addresses King Duncan is apologetic and submissive. She behaves this way to put the King at ease, and you know, probably to make him more susceptible to her husband's violence. Lady Macbeth plays both of these contrasting roles at the appropriate times in order to move the play in the direction which is most beneficial to her ambitions.

I can see I'm losing some of you because I bet many of you have your minds on last week's midterm, so let's end our discussion here today and go over your test, but next class, I want to pick up with the different styles of language Lady Macbeth uses to gain what she needs from the other characters in the play.

Listening Passage 2: Conversation Transcript

Narrator: Listen to a student and a professor discuss an independent study in translation.

Female student: Hello? Professor Anderson?

Female professor: Oh, hi Sally. Come on in. It'll be just a moment.

Female student: Alright, thank you.

Female professor: Let me find your file ... All right, here we are. You came in to talk to me about an independent study, correct?

Female student: Yes!

Female professor: Which subject is that for?

Female student: It would count as a credit towards advanced Italian since we don't have anything above intermediate this year.

Female professor: I know. Honestly, it's a shame that the previous professor had to step down, but we met up last week, and she said that her new job is going well.

Female student: That's great. She was my first-year professor, and she's the one who really got me excited about language study.

Female professor: I'm glad to hear that. Can you talk to me about your plan for this independent study?

Female student: I was hoping to do a translated collection of several short stories, all revolving around the theme of nature. I already have one or two that I want to work on, but I was hoping you could give me some recommendations for the others.

Female professor: Are you looking for stories that have already been translated or that have never been before?

Female student: I'm really looking for things that haven't been translated before and don't have a lot of literary critiques, so nothing too popular like Dante's *Divine Comedy*. I think retranslation is interesting, but I want to focus on more obscure texts that don't have much commentary yet.

Female professor: I understand. The *Divine Comedy* has been worked to death at this point. You might want to focus on more regional tales. Working with dialects may be difficult, but I think you'd be up to the challenge. Other than that, I recommend online publications that are always coming out with new works. I think I have a list of a few I can send to you.

Female student: That would be great. I also wanted to ask how an independent study with you will work. Will we meet every week? And what's the expectation for work for each meeting?

Female professor: It depends on how many credits you're applying for.

Female student: I'm thinking about applying for three credits.

Female professor: In that case, we would have a meeting once a week to discuss the work that you've done outside of our meeting times. The amount of work will depend on the text, I think, and how difficult it is to translate. You should come to our meetings prepared to talk about and present your work for at least an hour, but the specifics will be up to you.

Female student: That sounds great. Independent studies start in a week, right?

Female professor: That's correct. We can use our first meeting to talk more about your goals and decide on some of the stories you want to translate.

Female student: Thank you so much. I'll see you then.

LISTENING PASSAGE 3: LECTURE TRANSCRIPT

Narrator: Listen to part of a lecture on patterns of inheritance.

Female professor: All right, everybody. Last time, we talked about different modes of inheritance, which describe the way a trait is passed down from parent to child. Now, in this class, we are going to talk about a specific mode of inheritance: autosomal dominant inheritance. Let's break down what that means. First, let's talk about that word *autosome*. Does anyone in class remember the difference between autosomes and sex chromosomes? Yes, Kelly.

Female student: So, I think that autosomes are the numbered chromosomes that determine most of a person's characteristics, but a sex chromosome is what determines whether you are male or female, so like X and Y.

Female professor: Yes, you are exactly correct. Great job, Kelly. That's exactly it. A sex chromosome is a chromosome that determines a person's biological sex, and an autosome is any other chromosome. There are 22 pairs of autosomes, so they are numbered to make them easy to talk about. Autosomal traits are traits encoded by the genes found on one of the numbered chromosomes. Sex chromosomes also code for traits unrelated to sex, but sex-linked inheritance is a different mode of inheritance. Now, let's talk about what *dominant* means. Yes, Kelly?

Female student: Isn't there also another type called recessive?

Female professor: Yes, there are modes of inheritance involving dominant and recessive alleles, which are variations of genes. Those words are basically a way of showing how the traits interact with each other. A dominant trait will take precedence over a recessive trait. So, one single copy of a dominant allele is sufficient to pass on the trait to the offspring. But with recessive alleles, two copies are necessary for the person to express the trait. Can anyone think of a trait or disease that has an autosomal dominant pattern of inheritance? Jason.

Male student: Um, yeah. Isn't eye color—I mean brown eye color a dominant trait?

Female professor: Yes, Jason. You're right. Brown eye color is a trait dominant to blue eye color. Those who have blue eyes must have parents with blue eyes or their parents must be heterozygous, meaning that they have brown eyes but also carry a blue eye allele. Otherwise, it would not be possible. Many genetic diseases are passed down via an autosomal dominant modality, which means that only one copy of the mutated allele that causes the disease is sufficient to cause the disorder. With recessive disorders, however, um, two copies of the disease allele are necessary for the person to express the disorder. So, let's imagine a child, and one of their parents has an autosomal dominant disease, and that parent has only one copy of the disease allele. That means that the child has a 50 percent chance of having the disease. If both parents have one copy of the disease allele, then, what is the chance that the child will have the disease?

Male student: That would be a, um, 75 percent chance.

Female professor: Precisely. The child has a 75 percent chance of inheriting the dominant allele since they can get it from one or both parents. This is very different from autosomal recessive inheritance, a modality that requires two copies of the allele to be present. There has to be one from each parent as well. So, if there is one parent who has the disease, but the other parent does not and is not a carrier, the child would have a 0 percent chance of inheriting the disease. But if one parent has the disease, and the other parent is a carrier, that percentage jumps up to a 50 percent chance. If both parents are carriers, the child has a 25 percent chance of inheriting it. Now, one example of an autosomal dominant disorder is Huntington's disease. This is a neurodegenerative disorder caused by a mutation in one gene, called the Huntington gene. Individuals with a single copy of the allele will go on to develop this disorder. It's characterized basically by mood swings, violent behavior, and trouble with forgetfulness. And one of the big issues with Huntington's disease is that often the symptoms don't start showing up until the affected individual is around 30 to 50, which means they could have already had children and passed on the disorder without knowing it. This means that the disorder stays in the gene pool. But what about recessive disorders? How do they present in the population, and how prevalent are they?

Listening Passage 4: Lecture Transcript

Narrator: Listen to part of a lecture on classical conditioning.

Male professor: Good afternoon, class. It's nice to see you all today. So, last time we went over the concept of learning. Who can tell me what they remember about that?

Female student: Learning is like when you experience the environment.

Male professor: That's close. Learning is defined as some kind of behavioral change that results from an interaction with the environment. You were close but missing a few details because after the interaction or experience with the environment, the individual has to have a new configuration of responses to the external stimuli. That means what defines learning is a change in the way someone interacts with the environment. So, for example, if there was a child, and they encountered a dog that barked at them and made them feel afraid, the child may learn that the dog is frightening. Next time they see the dog, they are not going to approach the animal. This is what constitutes learning because, um, the child changed their behavior in response to an experience. Now, learning was widely studied by the behaviorists in the 1920s to 1950s. They defined learning as a set of observable changes in the behavior of a certain individual after they experienced a change in their environment, so just what I was talking about earlier with the dog. Uh, there are three main types of behavioral learning following the behavioral model: classical conditioning, operant conditioning, and modeling. Who here knows the most popular experiment with classical conditioning?

Male student: Isn't that—is this one Pavlov's dogs?

Male professor: Yes, it is. The most popular, the most well-known case of classical conditioning, or any conditioning, is that of Pavlov's dogs. Before we get into that experiment, let's focus on what classical conditioning is. It is essentially a way of learning where a stimulus is associated with a different stimulus that was previously neutral. And because of that association, the individual that is learning—the animal, the person—will respond in a certain way. So, in this case, the learning is completely subconscious and automatic, meaning that the individual is unaware of the change. In

Pavlov's experiment, he trained dogs to associate a neutral stimulus, the sound of a bell, with a different stimulus, that of food being shown. Because food was shown, the dogs salivated, and Pavlov wanted to see if he could associate the salivation with the bell instead of the presence of food. In order to do this, whenever he showed the dogs food, he rang the bell to make them unconsciously associate the sound of the bell with the food. Eventually, as a result of this conditioning, Pavlov was able to, uh, ring the bell without presenting food to the dogs, but they would still salivate. This kind of conditioning can also happen to people. Say you get food poisoning after eating chicken. It may not have been the chicken that made your body sick, but many people would be unable to eat chicken afterwards anyway. Can someone explain why this is an example of classical conditioning?

Female student: I think it's because the brain, uh, associated the idea of chicken with being sick after eating it.

Male professor: Exactly. The brain subconsciously decided that the chicken was responsible for feeling unwell and learned a response, which now makes you unable to enjoy chicken for the time being.

Listening Passage 5: Conversation Transcript

Narrator: Listen to a conversation about a final project and internship offer.

Male professor: Jennie? Are you free to talk about your botany lab reports?

Female student: Oh, yes. Is everything alright?

Male professor: Yes, I just wanted to let you know that you scored the highest grade in the class. Your lab journal was nearly 60 pages long, and the drawings were very detailed.

Female student: Thank you! I spent a lot of time working on it. Drawing and labeling the flowers was difficult sometimes, but I really enjoyed writing the labs.

Male professor: I could tell. Your project was one of the longest I've read so far. I know this class can be challenging, but I'm happy with how everyone has stepped up.

Female student: I agree. This class has been one of my favorites. I wanted to ask you a question about our final project as well. Is the lab open on the weekends for students to keep working on our herbarium specimens? I heard someone in class say that they couldn't get the door open, and I wanted to finish the final project early.

Male professor: Hmm. I emailed the college about that. The registrar said she had updated the permissions on my students' cards ... I'll send another email. You should come to campus this weekend and see if it works. If not, a security guard should be able to help you.

Female student: That was my plan anyways. I'm running out of time for all of my projects and wanted to finish as many as possible this weekend.

Male professor: Speaking of the end of the year, what are your plans for the summer?

Female student: I don't have many. I have an internship in the city, so I'm staying in the state, but that's only on the weekends.

Male professor: Would you be interested in working for the herbarium? One of my colleagues is looking for interns to work on his project. He's currently studying tomato plant gene mutations, but you'd also be helping around the lab.

Female student: That sounds amazing! What kind of work would I be doing? I've done some experiments in the chemistry department but nothing professionally.

Male professor: You would mostly be caring for the specimens, preparing DNA samples, and performing DNA analyses. Of course, you would be trained in how to use the equipment you haven't seen before.

Female student: All right. I think I can work with that.

Male professor: Great. The main goal of the study is to test how genetic variations in these plants affect their responses to different diseases. He's trying to pinpoint some of the genes that help them fight off the diseases, but he needs some interns to pick up some of the testing. We can talk more about the schedule as soon as your exams are over, but I'll let him know you're interested.

Female student: Thank you. That would be great.

Speaking Passage 1: Conversation Transcript

Narrator: Now listen to a conversation between two students.

Male student: Do you know why the library isn't open as late anymore?

Female student: Yeah, the head librarian stepped down. Didn't you see the announcement?

Male student: Oh, really? No. Wait, so how long are the hours reduced?

Female student: No one knows. They have to find a new librarian, so everyone's saying it'll be a month at least.

Male student: That's awful. Can't the school do anything to fix the problem?

Female student: I don't know. I know there's an interim head, but I think that's just enough to keep the library open.

Male student: The school should be doing more, especially for students who don't have other libraries to go to. Not to mention graduate students. They need access to the books in the campus library to write their theses.

Female student: Yeah, it's not convenient, but the school has scanned a lot of the books so that students can read them off campus.

Male student: That's great, but what about students who don't have Wi-Fi or internet connection at home? They have no way of accessing those books except in person. This is a huge step back for equity in the school.

Female student: I guess I didn't think about it that way. If I didn't have Wi-Fi at home, I wouldn't be able to write my essay that's due next week.

Male student: Exactly. And I'm sure there are lots of students who have jobs during the day too. The school just isn't providing for them.

SPEAKING PASSAGE 2: LECTURE TRANSCRIPT

Male professor: A psychologist named Albert Bandura conducted an experiment called the Bobo Doll Experiment to test whether observed behaviors would be imitated. There were 36 boys and 36 girls between three and six years old that were test subjects. The researchers for this experiment rated the children on their innate aggressiveness before the experiment began and formed groups based on these ratings. Of the three groups made, one was shown a model displaying aggressive behavior towards a toy, one saw a nonaggressive model, and the last group was the control group that had no model.

The results of this experiment were quite compelling. The children who were exposed to the aggressive model were far more aggressive than those in the nonaggressive or control groups.

SPEAKING PASSAGE 3: LECTURE TRANSCRIPT

Professor: OK class, settle down. Today, we're discussing an important aspect of language study called morphology. Morphological studies are focused on two main concepts: the structure of words and the changes made to words. But let's start smaller. A morpheme is the smallest unit of meaning in a language. Morphemes are not words by definition, although some free, or single, morphemes can be words. Morphemes may be free, existing alone, or bound, which means they are attached to, uh, another morpheme to form a word.

We'll continue with the two kinds of morphemes: lexical and grammatical. A lexical morpheme is the part of the word that carries intrinsic meaning, while the grammatical morpheme is the part that carries grammatical meaning. Let's take the word "dogs" for example. This word has two morphemes: "dog-" and "-s." The morpheme "dog" is lexical because it carries the meaning of a four-legged mammal. The morpheme "-s," however, does not have a, uh, inherent lexical value. Instead, this morpheme indicates that the word is plural. In languages other than English, like Italian and Spanish, a grammatical morpheme can also express gender.

Morphemes are important to the study of language because they determine the language's morphological category between isolating, fusional, agglutinative, and polysynthetic. We'll go into each of these categories more in-depth, but for now, simply note that the way morphemes are combined and expressed determines which category they fall under. For example, isolating languages like Mandarin rely principally on word order and context instead of grammatical morphemes to express meaning and grammar. These languages often contain free morphemes that have no grammatical indication. Finnish, on the other hand, is an agglutinative language, meaning it has combined lexical and grammatical morphemes to make words, but grammatical morphemes serve one purpose. In an agglutinative language, one grammatical morpheme may determine the word's number, but a separate morpheme is necessary to determine gender.

WRITING PASSAGE 1: LECTURE TRANSCRIPT

Female professor: I imagine that almost everyone here is at least familiar with the concept of an IQ test, or intelligence quotient test. While it's true that IQ tests have been popular for decades, scientists and psychologists have long since called into question their effectiveness. The purpose of IQ tests was originally to determine which students were falling behind academically, but these tests had—and have—greater cultural significance. Many people believe that a higher IQ means that a person is more intelligent than others, but this isn't true. IQ is not intelligence, because there are many ways to measure intelligence, and all IQ tests have their flaws. The problem with measuring human intelligence is that it is multifaceted and, more often than not, unable to be quantified in any real way. IQ can't span a lifetime, so the developers use certain, uh, criteria to determine question types and appropriate answers. So, one of the biggest issues with these tests is that they only test for those criteria and not the full range of human intelligence.

Alfred Binet, one of the developers of the Binet-Simon test, actually stated that his scale was not an accurate measure of intelligence but was instead a way to classify intellectual qualities. Even though his test was quite useful, it was never meant to quantify a person's mental capabilities. It was instead made to group individuals based on similar levels of intelligence ... specifically so that those who were falling behind could be more easily recognized. The Binet-Simon test was also criticized for not being culturally ubiquitous, meaning that questions would need to be modified in translation based on culture. This is a huge problem for other standardized tests as well like the Wechsler Intelligence Scale for Children, or WISC, which many scientists believe to be unreliable for certain ethnic or racial groups. A change proposed to remediate this issue resulted in the opposite as the scores of white children increased and the scores of those in minority groups decreased.

While many IQ tests like the WISC do correlate with higher academic performance, there is a lack of research on their correlation with the other aspects of intelligence. For example, Howard Gardner, a developmental psychologist, worked to define intelligence based on the necessary abilities for building culture. In 1983, he proposed the theory of multiple intelligences, which classified human intelligence into eight categories, including musical, interpersonal, nature, logic, words, bodily-kinesthetic, self, and picture. Categories like "word smart" and "logic smart" would be included on IQ tests, but other categories like "musical" or "self-intelligence" have no place in standardized IQ tests.

Gardner's theory stands in the face of the earlier tests seeking to quantify human intelligence since his theory is much less structured and objective. It also seeks to eliminate the cultural bias that is so prevalent in more standardized IQ tests. His theory, however, is also criticized but for the opposite reasons. Critics say that it is not based on empirical, or observed, evidence and that it is far too subjective to be considered an IQ test based in science.

Common English Language Idioms

- **A blessing in disguise** – a situation which at first seems bad, but which turns out to be a good thing.
    - "That red light was a blessing in disguise! If I hadn't stopped when I did, I would have been hit by another car."
- **A dime a dozen** – used when referring to something that is very common.
    - "The watch I have is really a dime in a dozen. I really want one that is unique!"
- **Beat around the bush** – to avoid talking about the main topic (usually one which is uncomfortable).
    - "Stop beating around the bush and just go tell her you like her."
- **Bite the bullet** – to face a problem or situation immediately rather than avoiding it.
    - "I want to ask for two weeks off from work but I am afraid to ask my boss. I guess I should just bite the bullet and ask her."
- **Break a leg** – said as a replacement for telling someone good luck.
    - "You'll do great at your performance. Break a leg!"
- **Call it a day** – to stop working for the day.
    - "I've made a lot of progress and I'm tired. I'm going to call it a day."
    - Can't make heads or tails of something – to not be able to understand something.
    - "I've read the example in the textbook three times and I still can't make heads or tails of it."
- **Couch potato** – a lazy person.
    - "You should stop being such a couch potato and go outside sometime."
- **Cut somebody some slack** – to allow someone to do something without judgment or hindrance.
    - "Cut him some slack! He worked all week and needs some time to relax."
- **Cutting corners** – to only do a job partially or to skip steps in the process.
    - "If you want to make good grades, you need to do the work thoroughly and not cut corners."
- **Don't count your chickens until (before) they hatch (they've hatched)** – to consider a payment or positive outcome as being yours before in possession.
    - "Don't buy something that expensive just because you think you'll be paid next month. You shouldn't count your chickens before they've hatched!"
- **Drag one's feet** – to delay doing something unpleasant.
    - "You should really go to the dentist for that toothache as soon as possible. Don't drag your feet!"
- **Egghead** – someone who is very intelligent.
    - "He makes straight As in all of his classes without even studying! What an egghead."
- **Elbow grease** – hard work or a high degree of effort (usually manual labor).
    - "Most household fixes don't need special tools; just a screwdriver and a little elbow grease will do it."

- **Easy does it** – a caution to be gentle or careful while performing a task.
    - "Set it down slowly. I don't want the piano damaged from moving it. Easy does it."
- **Feeling blue** – to be sad.
    - "Why are you sitting in the corner?"
    - "I'm just feeling a little blue today."
- **Fit as a fiddle** – to be healthy.
    - "I was sick for a couple of weeks, but now I'm as fit as a fiddle!"
- **Get something out of your system** – to do something so that you will not want or have to do it later.
    - "I really was feeling sad, so I cried for a while to get it out of my system."
- **Get your act together** – to recognize that the previous action was not good enough and try to do better.
    - "I've been skipping my reading every night and starting a bad habit. I need to get my act together starting today!"
- **Give someone the benefit of the doubt** – to trust someone without having a reason to do so.
    - "He wanted to borrow my truck, but I've never seen him drive. Maybe I should give him the benefit of the doubt and let him have it anyway."
- **Go back to the drawing board** – to have a failed first attempt and try to start over.
    - "Well, we tried and did not succeed. Time to go back to the drawing board."
- **Hang in there** – to persevere in a difficult or painful situation.
    - "Your job has been really hard lately, but you've done well to hang in there!"
- **Hit the sack** – to go to bed (usually early).
    - "I worked so hard today and am exhausted. I think I'll go ahead and hit the sack."
- **In over one's head** – to be in a situation that is too difficult to handle.
    - "I'm in a calculus class and don't understand anything. I think I'm in over my head."
- **It takes two to tango** – to state that it is more than one person's responsibility or fault (usually said in a negative way).
    - "She and I always fight about our relationship, but it's not all her fault. It takes two to tango."
- **It's not rocket science** – said about a relatively easy or simple task.
    - "You just have to water the flowers occasionally. It's not rocket science."
- **Jump the gun** – to rush or do something too early.
    - "I just couldn't wait! I jumped the gun and asked her to marry me last night."
- **Jump to a conclusion** – to make a judgment without hearing all of the evidence.
    - "She thinks I'm rich because she saw me wearing a suit and driving a nice rental car. If she saw what I normally drive, she wouldn't have jumped to that conclusion."
- **Just kidding** – something said to indicate that the previous statement was not true and was meant as a joke.
    - "She told me that she broke my phone, but then pulled it out and said 'just kidding!'"

- **Kill two birds with one stone** – to take care of two or more problems with one solution.
    - "We need to get a new phone and clothes, so let's just go to the mall later and kill two birds with one stone."
- **Let someone off the hook** – to no longer hold someone to doing something they had agreed to.
    - "My flight got cancelled, so you are off the hook for taking me to the airport."
- **Make a long story short** – to shorten or skip telling a story to reach the main point.
    - "To make a long story short, we had a really good time in our trip to London."
- **No pain, no gain** – said to indicate that doing something can be hard or even painful, but that it indicates progress.
    - "Running is so hard, but I have to do it. No pain, no gain."
- **On the ball** – to be ready or aware of what is happening.
    - "He always has the reading done ahead of the time. He's really on the ball."
- **Pull someone's leg** – used to indicate joking.
    - "I was pulling Susan's leg when I said I won the lottery."
- **Pull yourself together** – said to someone who is visibly emotional in an embarrassing way.
    - "You look like an emotional wreck! Pull yourself together."
- **Quick study** – used to describe someone who learns quickly.
    - "Everything comes so easily to Jim. He is such a quick study."
- **Rain or shine** – used to indicate that an event will happen no matter what happens. This does not necessarily apply to weather.
    - "We are going to watch that new movie on Friday, rain or shine!"
- **Rub the wrong way** – used to indicate that an action or person is irritating.
    - "He never seems like he is telling the truth and it really rubs me the wrong way."
- **So far, so good** – the work done up until this point has been done well.
    - "I'm halfway done with building my house and so far, so good."
- **Speak of the devil** – said when talking about a person and they show up. Can be positive or negative.
    - "Jim is such a nice guy!" (Jim then walks in) "Speak of the devil."
- **That's the last straw** – used to indicate that one too many bad things have happened.
    - "My boyfriend spilled coffee on me and constantly says mean things. The last straw, though, was when he broke my phone! I'm going to break up with him."
- **The best of both worlds** – to have the benefits of two situations that usually don't co-exist.
    - "She lives far enough away from the city that she can see the stars, but close enough to have a short commute. She really has the best of both worlds."
- **Time flies when you're having fun** – said when time seems to be going faster than normal while enjoying oneself.
    - "Our day at the theme park went by too quickly! Time flies when you're having fun."
- **To make matters worse** – usually used last in a list of bad experiences.
    - "I had a bad day. I stepped on a nail, ran out of gas, and to make matters worse, I still have to work tonight."

- **Under the weather** – used to say that someone is sick.
    - "I can't come to the party tonight; I'm under the weather. "
- **Vice versa** – used to indicate a reversal of two things in the previous statement.
    - "You earn money and then you can spend it, not vice versa."
- **We'll cross that bridge when we come to it** – putting off an issue for later.
    - "We somehow got the car to start this time, but we will have to fix it at some point. We will cross that bridge when we come to it."
- **Wrap your head around something** – to try to understand.
    - "Hey Jim, can you come and look at this?"
    - "Not right now, I'm trying to wrap my head around something."
- **You can say that again** – a statement used to indicate agreement to someone else's statement.
    - "I can't wait for payday."
    - "You can say that again!"
- **Your guess is as good as mine** – used to indicate a lack of knowledge.
    - "Hey, do you know which way it is to Peter's house?"
    - "Your guess is as good as mine!"
- **Zip your lip** – said to tell someone to be quiet.
    - "Hey! Zip your lip, the professor is talking."

How to Overcome Test Anxiety

Just the thought of taking a test is enough to make most people a little nervous. A test is an important event that can have a long-term impact on your future, so it's important to take it seriously and it's natural to feel anxious about performing well. But just because anxiety is normal, that doesn't mean that it's helpful in test taking, or that you should simply accept it as part of your life. Anxiety can have a variety of effects. These effects can be mild, like making you feel slightly nervous, or severe, like blocking your ability to focus or remember even a simple detail.

If you experience test anxiety—whether severe or mild—it's important to know how to beat it. To discover this, first you need to understand what causes test anxiety.

Causes of Test Anxiety

While we often think of anxiety as an uncontrollable emotional state, it can actually be caused by simple, practical things. One of the most common causes of test anxiety is that a person does not feel adequately prepared for their test. This feeling can be the result of many different issues such as poor study habits or lack of organization, but the most common culprit is time management. Starting to study too late, failing to organize your study time to cover all of the material, or being distracted while you study will mean that you're not well prepared for the test. This may lead to cramming the night before, which will cause you to be physically and mentally exhausted for the test. Poor time management also contributes to feelings of stress, fear, and hopelessness as you realize you are not well prepared but don't know what to do about it.

Other times, test anxiety is not related to your preparation for the test but comes from unresolved fear. This may be a past failure on a test, or poor performance on tests in general. It may come from comparing yourself to others who seem to be performing better or from the stress of living up to expectations. Anxiety may be driven by fears of the future—how failure on this test would affect your educational and career goals. These fears are often completely irrational, but they can still negatively impact your test performance.

Elements of Test Anxiety

As mentioned earlier, test anxiety is considered to be an emotional state, but it has physical and mental components as well. Sometimes you may not even realize that you are suffering from test anxiety until you notice the physical symptoms. These can include trembling hands, rapid heartbeat, sweating, nausea, and tense muscles. Extreme anxiety may lead to fainting or vomiting. Obviously, any of these symptoms can have a negative impact on testing. It is important to recognize them as soon as they begin to occur so that you can address the problem before it damages your performance.

The mental components of test anxiety include trouble focusing and inability to remember learned information. During a test, your mind is on high alert, which can help you recall information and stay focused for an extended period of time. However, anxiety interferes with your mind's natural processes, causing you to blank out, even on the questions you know well. The strain of testing during anxiety makes it difficult to stay focused, especially on a test that may take several hours. Extreme anxiety can take a huge mental toll, making it difficult not only to recall test information but even to understand the test questions or pull your thoughts together.

Effects of Test Anxiety

Test anxiety is like a disease—if left untreated, it will get progressively worse. Anxiety leads to poor performance, and this reinforces the feelings of fear and failure, which in turn lead to poor performances on subsequent tests. It can grow from a mild nervousness to a crippling condition. If allowed to progress, test anxiety can have a big impact on your schooling, and consequently on your future.

Test anxiety can spread to other parts of your life. Anxiety on tests can become anxiety in any stressful situation, and blanking on a test can turn into panicking in a job situation. But fortunately, you don't have to let anxiety rule your testing and determine your grades. There are a number of relatively simple steps you can take to move past anxiety and function normally on a test and in the rest of life.

Physical Steps for Beating Test Anxiety

While test anxiety is a serious problem, the good news is that it can be overcome. It doesn't have to control your ability to think and remember information. While it may take time, you can begin taking steps today to beat anxiety.

Just as your first hint that you may be struggling with anxiety comes from the physical symptoms, the first step to treating it is also physical. Rest is crucial for having a clear, strong mind. If you are tired, it is much easier to give in to anxiety. But if you establish good sleep habits, your body and mind will be ready to perform optimally, without the strain of exhaustion. Additionally, sleeping well helps you to retain information better, so you're more likely to recall the answers when you see the test questions.

Getting good sleep means more than going to bed on time. It's important to allow your brain time to relax. Take study breaks from time to time so it doesn't get overworked, and don't study right before bed. Take time to rest your mind before trying to rest your body, or you may find it difficult to fall asleep.

Along with sleep, other aspects of physical health are important in preparing for a test. Good nutrition is vital for good brain function. Sugary foods and drinks may give a burst of energy but this burst is followed by a crash, both physically and emotionally. Instead, fuel your body with protein and vitamin-rich foods.

Also, drink plenty of water. Dehydration can lead to headaches and exhaustion, especially if your brain is already under stress from the rigors of the test. Particularly if your test is a long one, drink water during the breaks. And if possible, take an energy-boosting snack to eat between sections.

Along with sleep and diet, a third important part of physical health is exercise. Maintaining a steady workout schedule is helpful, but even taking 5-minute study breaks to walk can help get your blood pumping faster and clear your head. Exercise also releases endorphins, which contribute to a positive feeling and can help combat test anxiety.

When you nurture your physical health, you are also contributing to your mental health. If your body is healthy, your mind is much more likely to be healthy as well. So take time to rest, nourish your body with healthy food and water, and get moving as much as possible. Taking these physical steps will make you stronger and more able to take the mental steps necessary to overcome test anxiety.

Mental Steps for Beating Test Anxiety

Working on the mental side of test anxiety can be more challenging, but as with the physical side, there are clear steps you can take to overcome it. As mentioned earlier, test anxiety often stems from lack of preparation, so the obvious solution is to prepare for the test. Effective studying may be the most important weapon you have for beating test anxiety, but you can and should employ several other mental tools to combat fear.

First, boost your confidence by reminding yourself of past success—tests or projects that you aced. If you're putting as much effort into preparing for this test as you did for those, there's no reason you should expect to fail here. Work hard to prepare; then trust your preparation.

Second, surround yourself with encouraging people. It can be helpful to find a study group, but be sure that the people you're around will encourage a positive attitude. If you spend time with others who are anxious or cynical, this will only contribute to your own anxiety. Look for others who are motivated to study hard from a desire to succeed, not from a fear of failure.

Third, reward yourself. A test is physically and mentally tiring, even without anxiety, and it can be helpful to have something to look forward to. Plan an activity following the test, regardless of the outcome, such as going to a movie or getting ice cream.

When you are taking the test, if you find yourself beginning to feel anxious, remind yourself that you know the material. Visualize successfully completing the test. Then take a few deep, relaxing breaths and return to it. Work through the questions carefully but with confidence, knowing that you are capable of succeeding.

Developing a healthy mental approach to test taking will also aid in other areas of life. Test anxiety affects more than just the actual test—it can be damaging to your mental health and even contribute to depression. It's important to beat test anxiety before it becomes a problem for more than testing.

Study Strategy

Being prepared for the test is necessary to combat anxiety, but what does being prepared look like? You may study for hours on end and still not feel prepared. What you need is a strategy for test prep. The next few pages outline our recommended steps to help you plan out and conquer the challenge of preparation.

Step 1: Scope Out the Test

Learn everything you can about the format (multiple choice, essay, etc.) and what will be on the test. Gather any study materials, course outlines, or sample exams that may be available. Not only will this help you to prepare, but knowing what to expect can help to alleviate test anxiety.

Step 2: Map Out the Material

Look through the textbook or study guide and make note of how many chapters or sections it has. Then divide these over the time you have. For example, if a book has 15 chapters and you have five days to study, you need to cover three chapters each day. Even better, if you have the time, leave an extra day at the end for overall review after you have gone through the material in depth.

If time is limited, you may need to prioritize the material. Look through it and make note of which sections you think you already have a good grasp on, and which need review. While you are studying, skim quickly through the familiar sections and take more time on the challenging parts.

Write out your plan so you don't get lost as you go. Having a written plan also helps you feel more in control of the study, so anxiety is less likely to arise from feeling overwhelmed at the amount to cover.

Step 3: Gather Your Tools

Decide what study method works best for you. Do you prefer to highlight in the book as you study and then go back over the highlighted portions? Or do you type out notes of the important information? Or is it helpful to make flashcards that you can carry with you? Assemble the pens, index cards, highlighters, post-it notes, and any other materials you may need so you won't be distracted by getting up to find things while you study.

If you're having a hard time retaining the information or organizing your notes, experiment with different methods. For example, try color-coding by subject with colored pens, highlighters, or post-it notes. If you learn better by hearing, try recording yourself reading your notes so you can listen while in the car, working out, or simply sitting at your desk. Ask a friend to quiz you from your flashcards, or try teaching someone the material to solidify it in your mind.

Step 4: Create Your Environment

It's important to avoid distractions while you study. This includes both the obvious distractions like visitors and the subtle distractions like an uncomfortable chair (or a too-comfortable couch that makes you want to fall asleep). Set up the best study environment possible: good lighting and a comfortable work area. If background music helps you focus, you may want to turn it on, but otherwise keep the room quiet. If you are using a computer to take notes, be sure you don't have any other windows open, especially applications like social media, games, or anything else that could distract you. Silence your phone and turn off notifications. Be sure to keep water close by so you stay hydrated while you study (but avoid unhealthy drinks and snacks).

Also, take into account the best time of day to study. Are you freshest first thing in the morning? Try to set aside some time then to work through the material. Is your mind clearer in the afternoon or evening? Schedule your study session then. Another method is to study at the same time of day that you will take the test, so that your brain gets used to working on the material at that time and will be ready to focus at test time.

Step 5: Study!

Once you have done all the study preparation, it's time to settle into the actual studying. Sit down, take a few moments to settle your mind so you can focus, and begin to follow your study plan. Don't give in to distractions or let yourself procrastinate. This is your time to prepare so you'll be ready to fearlessly approach the test. Make the most of the time and stay focused.

Of course, you don't want to burn out. If you study too long you may find that you're not retaining the information very well. Take regular study breaks. For example, taking five minutes out of every hour to walk briskly, breathing deeply and swinging your arms, can help your mind stay fresh.

As you get to the end of each chapter or section, it's a good idea to do a quick review. Remind yourself of what you learned and work on any difficult parts. When you feel that you've mastered the material, move on to the next part. At the end of your study session, briefly skim through your notes again.

But while review is helpful, cramming last minute is NOT. If at all possible, work ahead so that you won't need to fit all your study into the last day. Cramming overloads your brain with more information than it can process and retain, and your tired mind may struggle to recall even previously learned information when it is overwhelmed with last-minute study. Also, the urgent nature of cramming and the stress placed on your brain contribute to anxiety. You'll be more likely to go to the test feeling unprepared and having trouble thinking clearly.

So don't cram, and don't stay up late before the test, even just to review your notes at a leisurely pace. Your brain needs rest more than it needs to go over the information again. In fact, plan to finish your studies by noon or early afternoon the day before the test. Give your brain the rest of the day to relax or focus on other things, and get a good night's sleep. Then you will be fresh for the test and better able to recall what you've studied.

Step 6: Take a Practice Test

Many courses offer sample tests, either online or in the study materials. This is an excellent resource to check whether you have mastered the material, as well as to prepare for the test format and environment.

Check the test format ahead of time: the number of questions, the type (multiple choice, free response, etc.), and the time limit. Then create a plan for working through them. For example, if you have 30 minutes to take a 60-question test, your limit is 30 seconds per question. Spend less time on the questions you know well so that you can take more time on the difficult ones.

If you have time to take several practice tests, take the first one open book, with no time limit. Work through the questions at your own pace and make sure you fully understand them. Gradually work up to taking a test under test conditions: sit at a desk with all study materials put away and set a timer. Pace yourself to make sure you finish the test with time to spare and go back to check your answers if you have time.

After each test, check your answers. On the questions you missed, be sure you understand why you missed them. Did you misread the question (tests can use tricky wording)? Did you forget the information? Or was it something you hadn't learned? Go back and study any shaky areas that the practice tests reveal.

Taking these tests not only helps with your grade, but also aids in combating test anxiety. If you're already used to the test conditions, you're less likely to worry about it, and working through tests until you're scoring well gives you a confidence boost. Go through the practice tests until you feel comfortable, and then you can go into the test knowing that you're ready for it.

Test Tips

On test day, you should be confident, knowing that you've prepared well and are ready to answer the questions. But aside from preparation, there are several test day strategies you can employ to maximize your performance.

First, as stated before, get a good night's sleep the night before the test (and for several nights before that, if possible). Go into the test with a fresh, alert mind rather than staying up late to study.

Try not to change too much about your normal routine on the day of the test. It's important to eat a nutritious breakfast, but if you normally don't eat breakfast at all, consider eating just a protein bar. If you're a coffee drinker, go ahead and have your normal coffee. Just make sure you time it so that the caffeine doesn't wear off right in the middle of your test. Avoid sugary beverages, and drink enough water to stay hydrated but not so much that you need a restroom break 10 minutes into the test. If your test isn't first thing in the morning, consider going for a walk or doing a light workout before the test to get your blood flowing.

Allow yourself enough time to get ready, and leave for the test with plenty of time to spare so you won't have the anxiety of scrambling to arrive in time. Another reason to be early is to select a good seat. It's helpful to sit away from doors and windows, which can be distracting. Find a good seat, get out your supplies, and settle your mind before the test begins.

When the test begins, start by going over the instructions carefully, even if you already know what to expect. Make sure you avoid any careless mistakes by following the directions.

Then begin working through the questions, pacing yourself as you've practiced. If you're not sure on an answer, don't spend too much time on it, and don't let it shake your confidence. Either skip it and come back later, or eliminate as many wrong answers as possible and guess among the remaining ones. Don't dwell on these questions as you continue—put them out of your mind and focus on what lies ahead.

Be sure to read all of the answer choices, even if you're sure the first one is the right answer. Sometimes you'll find a better one if you keep reading. But don't second-guess yourself if you do immediately know the answer. Your gut instinct is usually right. Don't let test anxiety rob you of the information you know.

If you have time at the end of the test (and if the test format allows), go back and review your answers. Be cautious about changing any, since your first instinct tends to be correct, but make sure you didn't misread any of the questions or accidentally mark the wrong answer choice. Look over any you skipped and make an educated guess.

At the end, leave the test feeling confident. You've done your best, so don't waste time worrying about your performance or wishing you could change anything. Instead, celebrate the successful completion of this test. And finally, use this test to learn how to deal with anxiety even better next time.

Review Video: Test Anxiety
Visit mometrix.com/academy and enter code: 100340

Important Qualification

Not all anxiety is created equal. If your test anxiety is causing major issues in your life beyond the classroom or testing center, or if you are experiencing troubling physical symptoms related to your anxiety, it may be a sign of a serious physiological or psychological condition. If this sounds like your situation, we strongly encourage you to seek professional help.

Online Resources

Due to our efforts to try to keep this book to a manageable length, we've created a link that will give you access to all of your online resources:

mometrix.com/resources719/toefl-28244

It's Your Moment, Let's Celebrate It!

Share your story @mometrixtestpreparation